CW01558666

NAVIGA
RELATIONSHIPS
FOR LIFE

Setting an Intentional Course

Glenn C. Taylor

WHAT READERS ARE SAYING

"This book has deep roots and a solid foundation. I commend it to you."

Dr. Rod Wilson, Retired President, Regent College, Vancouver, B.C.

"This is a must read for anyone who is involved in ministry, counselling or leadership of any kind."

James Tughan, Executive Director, Semaphore Fellowship International, Artist, Oakville, Ontario

"How do we nurture life and love in one another?... How do we create communities of faith?... The reader is challenged to reflect on these questions... which enrich spiritually and enable growth both at a personal and communal level."

Diane Marshall, Psychotherapist, Toronto, Ontario

"In his book, Glenn posits a clarion call to address questions of isolation and loneliness by building up individuals, creating a healthy web of community and wholeness... inviting others to live, rather than to die."

Rev. Reid Cooke, Pastor and Chaplain, Niagara Falls, Ontario

"He weaves the web of nurturing others in the community of faith... insightful, handbook in positively influencing others."

Rev. David Johnson, Pastor, Hawkstone, Ontario

See full comments by all at the end of this book.

READ THIS FIRST!

Thank you for considering "Navigating Relationships for Life" This book is a distillation of my counselling ministiry ministry to many thousands of people over 60 years. It is one of a complete series "The Navigating Life Series." The other books in the series deal with various aspects of creating a truly successful life!

As a bonus I want to send you a complimentary resources on "Identifying and Managing Your Stress." It will take you less than 20 minutes to read. You can't get this anywhere else!

And it is FREE.

All you need to do is go to GlennCTaylor.ca/stress and tell us where to send it!

HTTPS://GLENNCTAYLOR.CA/STRESS

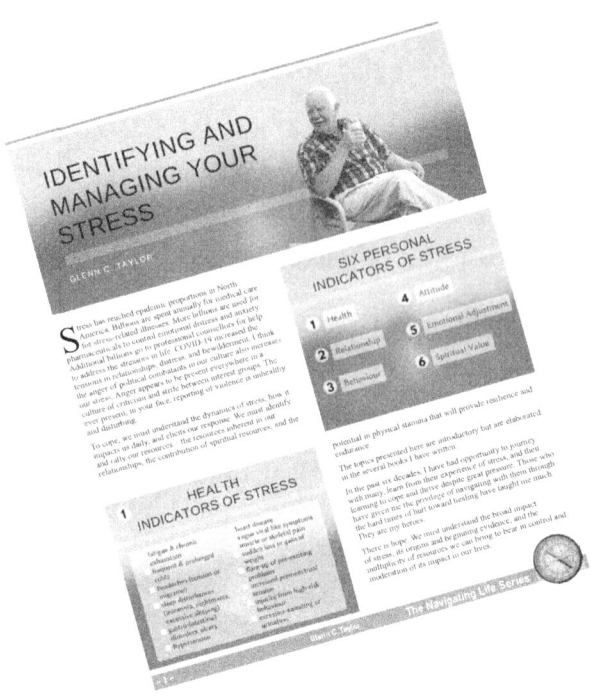

TABLE OF CONTENTS

What readers are saying 3

Preface and Art 7

Dedication 9

Acknowledgments and Introduction 11

Chapter One: The Web of Life 13
     Quality or Quantity 13
     Learning from Spiders 14
     Creating and Sustaining Our Web 15
     Community Is More Than Relational 16
     Impact: for Good Or Ill Is Reciprocal 17
     Explore and Interact 18

Chapter Two: The Power of Life and Death 21
     The Power of Speech 22
     Intentions and Outcomes 23
     The Wisdom Literature 24
     Invitations to Live Illustrated 25
     Invitations to Die Illustrated 26
     Our Personal Impact 27
     Explore and Interact 28
     Timothy's Reflection 29

Chapter Three: Nurturing Life In Others 31
     The Basics of Nurture 31
     The Invitation That Nurtures 32
     The Power of Invitation 33
     Life Initiating Phrases 34
     The Patterns of the Heart 35
     The Power of Gratitude 37
     The Art of Resuscitation 37
     Explore and Interact 38
     Timothy's Reflection 39

Chapter Four: Destroying Life in Others 41
    Response to Invitations to Die 41
    Sharpened Tongues and Drawn Swords 42
    Death by Friendly Fire 43
    Early Life Invitations to Die 45
    A Culture of Negativity 47
    Common Killer Phrases 48
    The Impact of Negativity 48
    Explore and Interact 50
    Timothy's Reflection 51

Chapter Five: A Place for Growth 53
    What to Do and Not Do 53
    Creating a Growth Environment 54
    The Will to Nurture 55
    Creating the Community for Growth 56
    Moving from Me to We 57
    Explore and Interact 61
    Timothy's Reflection 62

Chapter Six: The Tapestry of Christian Engagement 63
    The Tapestry of Participation in the Fellowship of Faith 63
    The Creation of a Culture of Commitment 64
    The Tapestry of Relationships 66
    The Tapestry of Behaviour 66
    Explore and Interact 69
    Timothy's Reflections 70

Chapter Seven: The Art of Navigating Relationships 73
    Exploring the Art 73
    Incarnating the Art 75
    The Complexity of the Art of Relating 76
    The Power for the Art 78
    Explore and Interact 79
    Timothy's Reflection 80

Endnotes 81

About the Author 84

Books by Glenn Calvin Taylor 85

What readers are saying 87

PREFACE AND ART

In all my contact with Glenn Taylor as a pastor, fellow-canoe tripper, and faculty member, one word I remember coming up repeatedly is "interdependence." The interconnectedness of us all in community is addressed in this book as either health-producing or as toxic, particularly in our interpersonal communication and especially our speech.

Supportive connections are everywhere in our lives. They appear in spider webs, social groupings, bridge structures, cloth weaving, rattan furniture, dam structures, etc. Connections provide strength and beauty. The beautiful poetry of his son, Tim, show thought connections through imagery.

In an age of perceived independence and self-expression at any cost, most modern art, as with any art throughout history, is in fact a witness to the complexity of language and its impact among us. The cover art for this book was created as one of a series of four liturgical banners in the style of Jackson Pollock, the great (and deeply troubled) American abstract expressionist. This work was painted by teenagers in a Canadian Vineyard Church under my direction and that of Heidi Brannan of the Semaphore Fellowship, a Christian visual art organization. It is a relational map that seems chaotic, but isolated within it, with squares and nimbus circles, isolated islands of nontoxic relationships with persons and with God. This is imaginative relational language translated into visual terms.

It is offered here, in support of Glenn's thesis that creativity, healthy growth and imagination itself are not an accident. It is a by-product of Biblically grounded, Spirit-guided empathic communication, full of grace and truth.

James Tughan

DEDICATION

To my wife, Mary Kathleen Taylor.

For over 65 years she has consistently

invited me to live.

Her affirmation, encouragement, and partnership

in ministry in many countries

has been sustaining and nurturing.

She is a "Wife of Noble Character."

Proverbs 31:10-31

ACKNOWLEDGMENTS AND INTRODUCTION

Relationships are essential to life and creativity. Scores of men and women have impacted my life. Many have invited me to live, to grow, to express myself, to learn to love, and to serve. At the centre of my life has been God's invitation to life and ministry. As a reluctant student and quite introverted person, he shook me with his love. Teachers, pastors, and friends have also encouraged me to enter the lives of others in multiple ways. They are far too numerous to mention. They know who they are, and I am grateful to them.

My wife and children, Dawn and Tim have been central in my support system. They have been active participants, accompanying me in other countries and coast to coast in Canada. They have filled my life with joy.

The theme of this book began to take shape in a psychiatric hospital where I researched a therapeutic community. Its uniqueness was in the expectation that everyone from the director to the youngest patient was expected to contribute to each person's life and well-being. For twelve years, I worked at implementing a "community philosophy" in a Bible College and for eight years sought to do the same in an inner-city ministry. Years working with juvenile delinquents reinforced how dramatically relationships shaped them.

Much of the content of this book was originally published as "The Web of Life." I have no doubt most authors have a desire to revise books written years earlier. Certainly, that is my experience. The book was well received but is not readily available in the original publication. Thus, this is my opportunity to revise, update and add to the basic thesis of the book. This has been a major re-write with significant additions to clarify the thesis.

Relationships impact each of us. The topography of life is full of valley and mountain experiences. The physical aspects of life which include health, sickness, losses, victories, and successes are important. However, the relational experiences in life are more crucial in their impact.

||||||||||||||||||||||||||||||||||||||||||||||||||||||||||||||||||||||||||||||||||||||||||||

The Relational topography outweighs the physical topography of life.

||||||||||||||||||||||||||||||||||||||||||||||||||||||||||||||||||||||||||||||||||||||||||||

Let me expand that claim. As children, we were taught to say, "Sticks and stones may break my bones, but names can never hurt me!" We knew it was not true! We were hurt by words. In addition to words there were many more ways to experience hurt. Were you ever chosen last as a team member? Rejection, attitudes, frowns, indeed, any form of put down, hurt a great deal. We are affirmed or denied significance in relationships.

The wounds of skinned knees, twisted thumbs, even cuts and bruises, healed more quickly than the relational hurts we experienced. Our sadness, sense of loss or feelings of rejection, all hurt more than the scrapes and physical injuries that were part of life. The wise man, Solomon, knew whereof he spoke when he said,

"The tongue has the power of life and death."[1]

Navigating the topography of relationships is a major problem in life. No one escapes unscathed from relationships. This book is about navigating relationships. Experiencing health and happiness in relationships and promoting the well-being of others in relationships is the essence of the interactions we experience. Each chapter will deal with a different aspect of this art of Canadian Artist and writer James Tughan who has written the Preface and the cover is the outcome of his work with youth defining relationships. James is a gifted and creative friend. I requested my son, Timothy, to prepare a poetic reflection on each chapter. He, along with my wife, Mary and daughter, Dawn, have been my relational strength.

Faith is also a relational anchor in my life. God invited me to live in Christ as a teen and has guided me in ministry for over 65 years in many countries and many cultures in the world. Truly in his Words, I have found life. This revision of the original book will elaborate some of that adventure in living at the invitation of so many people whom I have been blessed to know and to serve. It has been my privilege to invite others to live to our reciprocal benefit. The individual is too small a container for all that life has to offer. We share with others and grow thereby.

CHAPTER ONE: THE WEB OF LIFE

Words change in meaning over time. "Web" has new meaning today. Electronics has created a new web, expanding our options for relating to each other. We talk of "friends" and "hits" as a measure of connectedness. Connections are relationships. The web provides the environment in which we interact, communicate, play, debate or express love.

The web is affecting people in ways not before dreamed of by most people. It leads to the development of relationships that are based on anonymous connections. That is, connection to people we do not know nor know if we can trust. Today according to much research youth especially are influence in ways not before conceived. They are being influenced by individual with very different values. Sometimes the changes are affected by people with hidden agendas or individuals seeking parasitic relationships. There is no community in these relationships because of the superficial nature of this form of connection. Misinformation is rampant and it is influential. The rise of a sense of loss of community among youth who spend much time in "web relationships" is very significant. This web does not meet our social, emotional, relational, or spiritual needs. Instagram is only one of the most common forms of this web phenomenon.

Quality or Quantity

The level of engagement can be measured in many ways. The number of electronic "friends" may express different levels of intimacy. It may simply mean the exchange of information. It may evidence minimal intimacy or different strengths of relationship. Consider the difference between sharing factual information and sharing meaning of an emotional significance. The friends I have on a team in sports will involve a different level of commitment. Someone who comforts me in sickness or celebrates with me in success are different forms of connection.

Solomon captures the difference,

> *"There are three things that are too amazing for me, four that I do not understand: the way of an eagle in the sky, the way of a*

*snake on a rock, the way of a ship on the high seas, and the way
of a man with a young woman."*[2]

The mystery of love separates intimacy and acquaintance. The strength of connection varies from situation to situation. However, all of our relationships are part of our web of life.

||||||||||||||||||||||||||||||||||||||||||||||||||||||||||||||||||||||||||||||||||||||||||

There is mystery in our web of relationships.

||||||||||||||||||||||||||||||||||||||||||||||||||||||||||||||||||||||||||||||||||||||||||

Think of your favorite TV drama with the complexity, intrigue, tensions, and manipulations that create the drama of relationships. Life is like that. The range of options in our engagements with others is infinite. They are crucial to our existence and the creators of our pain and joy day by day. Even if we have quantity of relationships, we long for quality, depth, meaning, and significance. The hunger in each of us for connection is acute. Pain or pleasure in relationship creates meaning in life.

Learning from Spiders

Like spiders we create intricate webs that are complex, durable and fulfill purposes in our lives. Our webs are living things. They grow, move, change, sway in the breezes of life. They may seem tenuous but have amazing strength and resilience. We are richer or poorer based on the webs we create for our lives.

The spider is a masterful creator of webs. Maybe you don't like spiders or, perhaps you have experienced their sticky web. I've never met anyone with a pet spider. However, they have much to teach us. The little rhyme about the "itsy bitsy spider" going up the waterspout speaks to their persistence and commitment in their creativity. Rain or shine, they get the job done! The industrious spider certainly could compete with the ant.

When you touch the web at any point, it sets the whole web trembling. That vibration signals that the web has caught the intended prey, a meal for the hungry spider. The silk web is dispersed through a spinneret of which there are seven types varying from species to species. The strength of the silk is roughly equivalent to that of high-grade alloy steel of similar dimensions. The spider casts the strands which are carried by the breeze to attach itself, thus, becoming a highway for movement and further casting of the web. The web sits quietly to catch its prey which will be wrapped in silk to immobilize for the spider's meal.

We, too, cast our webs seeking attachment. Our webs increase in strength through continuing contact and repletion in relationships that become strong through usage. Our webs are as sensitive as those of the spider. When our web is touched for good or ill it trembles and the movement spreads through our web of relationships. The loss or gain of one friend may expand or contract by the engagement with others. In a new social environment, we may cast about for relationships to reduce our sense of aloneness or isolation. We may fish for contacts on the web to expand our involvement. We may do this with tentativeness or in seeking those of common interests.

Creating and Sustaining Our Web

Studies indicate that even in the fetal stage the web of life is beginning to take shape. In early childhood, relational patterns form. Social patterns take shape early. Messages received may be largely non-verbal. Sensitivities are acute in children long before verbal skills develop. Socialization enhances or inhibits the facility of web development. Security is a key issue for children leading to facility in reaching out or withdrawing from relational contact. Curiosity is either enhanced or inhibited. Teasing, bullying, and insulting are impactful. Affirmation, encouragement, and warmth equally shape the child.

The web of life is shaped. Without intentional change, patterns retain consistency into adulthood. Relationships are central to human existence. The influence of others may be positive or negative and may be very dramatic in impact. There is no isolated existence. You may recall the poem of John Donne,

> "No man is an island,
> Entire to itself,
> Every man is a piece of the continent,
> A part of the main.
> If a clod be washed away by the sea,
> Europe is the less…
> Any man's death diminishes me,
> Because I am involved in mankind,
> And therefore never send to know for whom the death tolls;
> It tolls for thee."[3]

All people are connected. In the Biblical record, it becomes obvious that no person was to stand alone. Adam required Eve for completion. God called Abraham to become a great nation, a community of faith. Jesus saw persons as related in love and unity and prayed that his followers would become one in relationships of mutual edification. In the fourth century, Julian of Norwich captured this in these words, "For when I look to myself as a single individual, then I am nothing. But all my hope comes from being united in one love with all my fellow Christians."[4]

Twentieth century martyr for his faith, Bonhoeffer, wrote, "Let him who cannot be alone beware of community… Let him who is not in community beware of being alone."[5] We come to know ourselves best in relationship with others.

The community with others is God's provision for self-discovery. We are reflected back to ourselves in the perspective of others. Our true selves are reflected in the mirror of social relationships. Learning is possible with humility in listening. Sydney Jourard, a psychologist of the past century, declared, "And it seems to be another empirical fact that no man can come to know himself except as an outcome of disclosing himself to another person…The man who is alienated from his fellows is alienated from himself. Alienated man is not known by his fellows, he doesn't know himself."[6] Feedback from others is essential. We cannot function as if we are the only one. Every life touches another. The question becomes whether our touch is positive or negative.

Psychiatrist, Roberto Assagioli, puts the point strongly. "The isolated individual does not exist, every person has intimate relationships with other individuals which make them all interdependent."[7] This interdependence is the heart of community where we care for each other. My preferences must be modified by the needs of others. Our belonging reaches back to our family and our responsibility reaches forward to future generations.

Community Is More Than Relational

The individual cannot exist in isolation. Our western approach to individuality, individual rights, self-fulfillment has led us to an "atomistic" view of the person. Canadian philosopher, Charles Taylor deals with this extensively. The human capacity for autonomy or self-actualization is a fiction. Individuals are nurtured by others from birth. Adulthood does not free us from the need for others. We may give another freedom of expression but isolation in autonomy is not a real possibility for persons. This interdependency is not simply relational, but most importantly, spiritual.

Despite the emphases in Christianity on individual salvation, the Scripture teaches that we are intimately dependent. The imagery of the New Testament focuses on the corporate dependency in the analogy of the relationship of believers being a community of faith, an assembly, a body, and a vine. Isolation in autonomy is a concept foreign to Biblical teaching. Indeed, the responsibility we have in relation to one another is of extreme importance in the community of faith. Leadership never replaces each believer's responsibility for other believers. An individual may have individual faith but will express that faith in relation to others.

IIIIIIIIIIIIIIIIIIIIIIIIIIIIIIIIIIIIIIIIIIIIIIIIIIIIIIIIIIIIIIIIIIIIIIIIIIIIIIIIIIIIIIIIIII

Relationships are the essence of being human.

IIIIIIIIIIIIIIIIIIIIIIIIIIIIIIIIIIIIIIIIIIIIIIIIIIIIIIIIIIIIIIIIIIIIIIIIIIIIIIIIIIIIIIIIIII

Impact: for Good Or Ill Is Reciprocal

Our lives are touched by parents, siblings, teachers, athletic coaches, friends, playmates who help to define ourselves to ourselves. I wanted to be like my Uncle Charlie. He was tall, quiet, dignified and while sitting quietly smoking his pipe after a meal exuded confidence. It was quieting to be in his presence, a peaceful time. On the other hand, in a one-room elementary school, I had difficulty with spelling due to a learning disability. We received the strap for too many mistakes in spelling. I felt like crawling under the carpet, embarrassed and humiliated. I was invited to live in Uncle Charlies presence and invited to die by that teacher. One touched my life positively and one negatively.

While writing this chapter, I watched *American Idol.* As Kelly Clarkson sang her song, *"Piece by Piece"*, I was moved to tears. Feeling rejected by her father as a six-year-old she wrote,

> "All I remember is your back
> Walking toward the airport, leaving us all in your past
> I travelled fifteen hundred miles to see you
> Begged you to want me, but you didn't want to…"

It was a powerful rejection, redeemed by her husband of who she wrote,

> "But piece by piece, he collected me
> Up off the ground, where you abandoned things, yeah
> Piece by piece he filled the holes that you burned in me
> At six years old and you know, he never walks away
> He never asks for money, he takes care of me
> He loves me
> Piece by piece, he restored my faith
> That a man can be kind and a father could…stay."

Here was a real and artistically presented illustration of an invitation to die and an invitation to live. Her web of life was set atremble by two who touched her differently. We desperately need the blessing that is experienced in the touch of others. We yearn for such a touch. I recall the pleading of Esau who was cheated out of a blessing by his brother Jacob. Esau pleaded,

"Bless me too, my father!"[8]

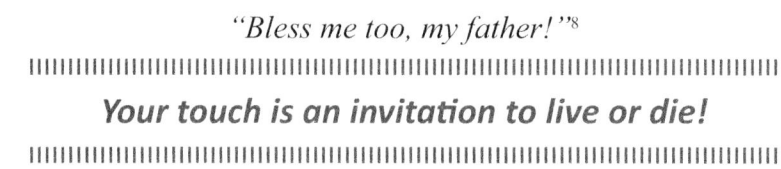

Your touch is an invitation to live or die!

When ministering in Africa, it became important for me to administer a test that required each person to answer the questions for themselves. Reflecting my Canadian culture, I explained that there was to be no cheating. As they began to complete the form, they proceeded to share answers with each other. I stopped the process and asked what it meant to cheat. The answer given to me was, "To cheat is to withhold what would be helpful to another." Thus, not to cheat was to share answers so everyone succeeded.

We cheat others by inviting them to die by discouraging, rejecting, turning away from, or insulting others. We invite others to live by affirming, encouraging, helping, building others, expressing love and gratitude. The choice is ours. We are not neutral in our relationships. In our relationships we touch each other's lives in helpful or harmful ways. Explore these possibilities with me in this adventure of touching the lives of each other. We will explore ways to measure our impact and to bring healing to each other.

Explore and Interact

1. Who provided the most impact on your life during each decade – positive and negative?

Person of Impact

Decade	Positive	Negative
0s		
10s		
20s		
30s		
40s		
50s		
60s		
70s		

Decade	Positive	Negative
80s		

2. Do you tend to see yourself as an island, peninsula, or part of a continent. Do you wish one to be stronger than another, or to change?

Self-Identification

Island	Peninsula	Continent

3. Identify a couple of "shaping events" in your life, either positive or negative. List the "touches" for which you are especially grateful which where an invitation to grow, to live, and to celebrate your being.

Experiences for Gratitude

TIMOTHY'S REFLECTION

I dreamed of my assembly

Friends and family
Placed bricks as puzzle pieces
Of whom I would be
Yet some
Removed bricks
Of whom I might have been.

I watched myself grow and shrink
Finding sincerity of task elusive.

Who care most for me?

Some pieces were laid with attention
It was easy to behold.

Some were very poorly laid
And favored the constructor
And their ease of placement.

Yet, some were beautiful
And made me proud to be

As my construction matured
It also slowed
I felt a loss of control
Of who I was
Who I was meant to be

It was shocking
That most of my structure
Was determined
By words

I wondered at
The Architect
All the while attending
The construction
And demolition
Of others
By my own words.

CHAPTER TWO: THE POWER OF LIFE AND DEATH

The words of Solomon were quoted earlier,

"The tongue has the power of life and death, ... "[9]

In the context it speaks of the "*... the harvest of their lips ... .*" The tongue is an instrument of communication. Our communication produces a harvest. Jesus speaks of the fruit of a tree being good or bad. He uses this analogy to say,

"For the mouth speaks what the heart is full of. ... By your words you will be acquitted, and by your words you will be condemned."[10]

It is obvious that the tongue is only the instrument of something much deeper.

We hear words with our ears. However, words express deeper meanings. These are conveyed by emotion, tone, gestures, the eyes, and body posture. There may be discrepancies between these levels of communication. Words express only a part of the message and, in themselves, may be a diversion or fail to express all the intent. These deeper dimensions of communication may convey the invitation to live or to die.

In addition to different dimensions of expression involved in communicating, there are different depths or levels of communication. One may communicate at the level of cliché conversation which is a social interaction, simply state the facts, or a deeper level that expresses personal meaning or emotional significance. Deeper levels are more risk sensitive as one is revealing personal importance of the expression.

Communication

Dimensions	Levels
• Verbal content	• Cliche content
• Gestures	• Just the facts
• Tonal content	• Personal meaning
• Emotional content	• Personal judgement

One can readily see that communication involves many factors. This is what makes it so powerful in its ability to communicate life or death. The power of language is immense. It impacts our lives constantly in our social interaction with others. It is no exaggeration to say that the power of life and death are in the tongue. The power of our speech is impactful.

The Power of Speech

There is great power in speech. Those of us who remember the Second World War may remember the power of Churchill's oratory. No one who heard Churchill's challenge in 1940 will forget his offer of "Blood, Toil, Tears and Sweat." Nor do Americans forget Patrick Henry declaration in 1775, "Give me liberty or give me death." Another great orator was Hitler who was effective in swaying and shaping the minds of people toward his objectives. In 1937, A. E. Frauenfeld, writing in German said, "Seldom in the history of the German people, indeed that of human-ity itself, did the spoken word, that direct personal contact between the leader of a young and rising movement and the whole people, have such importance as in this significant period in the history of the German people."[11] There is great power in our words for good or ill. The impact of words is vast. They may be toxic or tender, encourage to living or surrender, affirm or affront, invite to live or invite to die. The power of life and death are in our words to each other.

The affirmation of my father was crucial for me. It elevated my joy, well-being and self-confidence. My maturity scale went up when he said, "Son, I believe you will make the right decision and I'll support you." I went to him for input. He helped me clarify the factors involved but, then, assured me that he believed I would make the best decision. On the other hand, I had some teachers who were very negative. They made me feel dumb or incompetent, inviting me to die. The tongue is key in the dynamic of relationships.

This understanding raises the power of speech to a high level of importance. Fredrick Buechner captures this, "As we move around this world and as we act with kindness perhaps, or with indifference or with hostility toward the people we meet, we are setting the great spider web atremble. The life that I touch for good or ill will touch anther life, and that in turn another, until who knows where the trembling stops or in what far place my touch will be felt."[12]

The fruit of communication may be good or evil. Our speaking touches others like missiles in a war zone. They are powerful when personal but also may reach a great distance. What is the effect of my touch? Remember touch is not simply physical. We touch people with our verbal expression and our attitude. There is reciprocal effect. We may be invited to die, and we may invite others to die. The power of our touch on others is dramatic, as is theirs on us. We are both recipients and dispensers of this toxic injection of poison.

||||||||||||||||||||||||||||||||||||||||||||||||||||||||||||||||||||||||||||||||||||||||||||||||

The tongue is dynamic in relationships.

||||||||||||||||||||||||||||||||||||||||||||||||||||||||||||||||||||||||||||||||||||||||||||||||

A dramatic illustration of the impact of words or physical relationship is constantly reported in the news. Many times, we have heard of youth who have committed suicide in response to the negative imparting of words through texting, insulting, Facebook, or on the school grounds. When people receive the message of rejection they personalize the message in despair. Death by one's own hands in suicide is a common response of youth to invitations to die. The suggestions, "Why don't you kill yourself?"; "You are of no value to anyone!"; "You're a waste of space!" These are taken seriously with dire consequences.

Intentions and Outcomes

An off-handed comment may have unintended outcomes. How often have you, in response to an unintended reading of your expression said, "Oh, that's not what I intended!" We may not intend our gesture or tone to convey rejection, but it frequently does. We may be preoccupied and respond without thinking to a child. Sometimes my son would ask me something when I was deep in thought. I would grunt a response, without thought, to what for him was a crucial question of importance.

Occasionally, our words may not be understood. When two grandsons at pre-school age visited us at a new property for the first time, we had such an incident. My wife explained that they must not go to the pond without an adult. Very soon, she looked out the window to find them at the pond. They were in danger. After scolding, they were sent out to play. Shortly thereafter the older came to me. The conversation went like this,

"Grampa, can I ask you question?"

"Sure."

"What is an adult?"

The children would have known what a "big person" or "parent" meant, but the word "adult" had no meaning to them. My wife's instruction was not understood. The children's intention was not to disobey. There were misunderstanding all around. Miscommunication can lead to invitations to die.

Yes, sometimes we do mean harm with words or actions. Cutting comments, harsh accusations, injurious judgments, lying responses are all invitations to die. On the other hand, comforting, encouraging, affirming, or thoughtful comments are intentional invitations to life. It requires courage to examine our expressions and our intentions. As the Scripture says,

"For the mouth speaks what the heart is full of."[13]

Understand the impact of words and actions requires self-examination

It may be unintentional but still harmful. Both the sender of the message and the recipient may need examination. Yes, sometimes we are too sensitive. Our response may be an indication of where we are within ourselves. When I am feeling down, I may be much more sensitive and interpret things too personally or negatively. Others may not intend to be oppositional. In sending messages, we may be speaking out of our pain or hurt. Even emotions with which we are not aware may lead to unintended expression that are hurtful. There is a reciprocity in giving and receiving messages. We may be reactive. My father taught us a saying, instructing us through an axiom to be careful. He said some people's response is, "You kill my dog, I'll kill your cat!" He urged us not to be retaliatory in our response. Examining this "expression-response" equation from both ends may be very instructive. The artistry of communication requires examination and learning.

The Wisdom Literature

The Wisdom Literature in the Old Testament bears witness to the impact of our behaviour and words have on each other.

"Anxiety weighs down the heart, but a kind word cheers it up."[14]

"The tongue of the wise adorns knowledge, ..."[15]

"Gracious words are a honeycomb, sweet to the soul and healing to the bones."[16]

Regardless of how secure we feel in ourselves, when confronted by anxiety, we feel weighed down. Similarly, when receiving a good word, a wise and helpful suggestion, or pleasant words, we are lifted in spirit. We walk with a lighter step. Indeed, physiologically this can be measured. Our emotions determine our physiological state. The lie detector test is based on this technology. A friend completed a doctoral thesis focusing on the changes in the eyes in response to emotional states. The body does not lie, even though our words may do so. As a professional counselor, it is important to me to read the visual clues provided by the body. The invitation to live or die is fully evidenced by the body, even if we are not conscious of the evidence of our response.

The response of the body is much more adequate and reliable than our emotions or even our reason. As someone has said, "The body keeps the score, the body does not lie." Our emotions may be confused by our desires for connection with others, or the impact of not feeling well. We have all experienced making decisions under duress of many kinds. The physiological response of the body is subconscious, a function of the autonomic nervous system and the chemistry of the body. It usually quite accurately reflects what we are experiencing emotionally even when we rationally tell ourselves something different. As illustrated above, anxiety feels weighty but encouragement in pleasant words is sweet like honeycomb

Invitations to Live Illustrated

The conversation between God and Abram illustrates this.

> *"... the word of the Lord came to Abram in a vision: 'Do not be afraid, Abram. I am your shield, your very great reward.' But Abram said, 'Sovereign Lord, ... I remain childless and the one who will inherit ...' And Abram said, 'You have given me no children; ... Then the word of the Lord came to him: 'This man will not be your heir, but a son who is your own flesh and blood will be your heir.'"*[17]

This promise brought new life and hope to Abram. He later was named Abraham and was to become the father of many nations. God's words brought new energy, hope and faith to Abraham.

Joseph invited his brothers to live. They had betrayed him andsold him into slavery. Later, they came to him and to be rescued from starvation in fear and trembling they stood before him. His words not only rescued them from starvation but from fear of retaliation. He said,

*"But God sent me ahead of you to preserve for you a remnant
on earth and to save your lives by a great deliverance. ... I will
provide for you ..."*[18]

These were words of life to the brothers. They expected deserved punishment but received forgiveness – not only in words but with the action of hugging and celebration. This was an invitation to life rather than the sentence of death.

Jonathan, despite his father who wished David's death, invited David to live.

*"... Jonathan went to David at Horesh and helped him find
strength in God. 'Don't be afraid,' he said. 'My father Saul will
not lay a hand on you. You will be king over Israel, and I will be
second to you.'"*[19]

Their mutual support is a classic illustration of one person putting his life on hold for the sake of another. Johathan put David's interests ahead of his own, inviting him to live. Saul was literally trying to take David's life.

When the Apostle Paul was discouraged and depressed, Titus came to refresh him. Paul declares,

*"... we had no rest, but we were harassed at every turn –
conflicts on the outside, fears within. But God, ... comforted us
by the coming of Titus, ..."*[20]

The refreshment of Titus invited Paul to life and joy, rescuing him from depression.

Invitations to Die Illustrated

Hear what the Old Testament says about invitations to die.

*"They sharpen their tongues like swords and aim cruel words
like deadly arrows."*[21]

"How long will you torment me and crush me with words?"
said Job who also spoke of *"... the lash of the tongue, ..."*[22]

"The words of the reckless pierce like swords, ..."[23]

*"I am in the midst of lions; I am forced to dwell among
ravenous beasts – men whose teeth are spears and arrows,
whose tongues are sharp swords."*[24]

||||||||||||||||||||||||||||||||||||||||||||||||||||||||||||||||||||||||||||||||||||||||
Tongues are lethal weapons.
||||||||||||||||||||||||||||||||||||||||||||||||||||||||||||||||||||||||||||||||||||||||

We can never fully understand the motives of others. Job's friends came to him with good intentions of comfort and did so for several days as they silently sat with him. However, they ended up inviting him to die. He felt misunderstood, betrayed, judged, and rejected. He became, as we often do, defensive. Their pious platitudes seemed unreal and like judgment to him. Quite literally, Joseph's brothers invited him to die because of jealousy and the favoritism of his father toward him. He invited them to live in reconciliation. The art of inviting each other to live or die is as old as humanity. Whether with mockery, sarcasm, put-downs, or bullying, we artfully invite each other to die.

Our Personal Impact

Cartoons and TV programs illustrate this. Lucy tricked Charlie Brown by offering to hold the football while he kicked it, only to move it at the last second. Archie Bunker constantly abused Meathead, his son-in-law, with put-downs. You have seen that in Everybody Loves Raymond or The Big Bang Theory.

Language is rarely neutral. The important question is, what is your style in relating to others? We need to look deeply into our souls with honesty. We say that actions speak louder than words. However, we cannot deny the power of words. Communication is the transfer of meaning. In the book of Proverbs, there are more than thirty references to the quality and impact of our speech. Job was quite descriptive of the speech of his friends,

> *"Will your long-winded speeches never end? What ails you that you keep on arguing? I also could speak like you, if you were in my place; I could make fine speeches against you and shake my head at you. But my mouth would encourage you; comfort from my lips would bring you relief. Yet if I speak, my pain is not relieved; and if I refrain, it does not go away."* [25]

He felt crushed by their words and actions.

Jesus used an analogy of the tree and its fruit,

> *"Each tree is recognized by its own fruit. ... For the mouth speaks what the heart is full of."* [26]

Our style has an impact peculiar to us. It is helpful for us to look in the mirror and seek to understand our impact on others. We do have the power of life and death. It resides in our tongue that instrument of communication. We will next explore those things that nurture us in our relationship to each other.

Explore and Interact

1. Identify a couple of occasions when your expression did not represent well your intention.

2. Illustrate how you have been invited to live or die as a child, adolescent, or an adult. Was this in a family experience, an educational, or vocational context?

3. What type of speech – anger, sarcasm, criticism, encouragement, compliment – affects you most? Illustrate.

TIMOTHY'S REFLECTION

"You are the strongest person I have ever met."
said the coach
to the small thin boy
who couldn't manage
a single pushup.
"You are the strongest person I have ever met."
she said to the chubby girl
who faltered before her
as she laughed.

"You are the strongest person I have ever met."
said the bride
as she vowed to her new husband,
teary eyes filled with joy.

The small thin boy dreamed
of size
that never came.

The chubby girl
shrank to unnoticeable
trepidation.

And the husband
was the strongest person
the wife had ever met.

CHAPTER THREE: NURTURING LIFE IN OTHERS

We begin life with a clear and unambiguous need for nurture. No baby would survive without nurture. You may have heard of the condition of some babies called, "failure to thrive." It occurs when the child does not experience touch, cuddling, warmth and nurture of another person immediately after birth. It occurred in nurseries of abandoned children where adequate care was not provided. The same lack of thriving occurs in youth or adults who do not experience adequate nurture.

The Basics of Nurture

Touch, communication, warm relationships, affirmation, encouragement, comfort, and challenge accompanied by the offer of assistance are basics. But the most basic element is simply presence – the art of being present in another's life, even if only with silence. These constitute the art of inviting others to live. We are all capable of providing these for each other. You have the power in speech, actions, attitude, and just being there for others to invite others to live! What a gift to be able to offer to others.

A personal illustration may help. Growing up in a survival family during the Second World War, it was necessary for children to contribute to family survival. For my older siblings this meant going out to work immediately after elementary school. Being one of the younger boys, and not being needed to support the family, I was offered the opportunity to go to secondary school. My parents told me I had a choice – work or continue schooling. I did not know anyone who had gone to school beyond elementary school and did not consider it of value. However, I decided to take the risk. It did not work out well. I soon tired of school and decided to quit and find a job.

My parents accepted my decision. However, the principal, Mr. McGill, did not. Two days after I quit my mother received a phone call from Mr. McGill. The conversation went like this,

Mr. McGill, "Mrs. Taylor, where is Glenn, I heard he wanted to quit school?"

Mom, "Yes, he decided to quit and is out looking for work."

Mr. McGill. "When he sets foot in your door, please tell him I want him back in high school. He has the ability to do the work and needs to complete his schooling. I want him back right away! He can succeed."

Need I tell you that when I came home three days later, I started school again the next day. Maybe a little background would help. School was not a good experience for me. A learning limitation involving the inability to replicate the sounds I hear was part of it. My rebellion was a bigger part. A couple of teachers seem to me to be abusive, and I talked back to them. They sent me to the principal's office. Thus, I came to know Mr. McGill and he knew me. His discipline was fair, immediate, just, and administered with humor. I liked him. When he told me he wanted me back in school and, especially, his claim that I had the ability, I had no choice but to return. I completed secondary school. I wish I could tell him I went to school for many more years. It was because he invited me to live. He saw beyond my disinterest and rebellion and affirmed me. What an invitation to live! He nurtured me and started me on a great adventure of learning and service which would have been unlikely without his invitation to live. Now, that is nurture!

The Invitation That Nurtures

Invitations identify possibilities, express expectations, create hope, see beyond limitations, infuse motivation, and affirm dreams. They also create dreams that reach beyond immediate obstacles. This was what Mr. McGill did for me. Scripture refers to words that are apt, timely, discerning, cheerful, kind, healing, gentle, careful, just. These are words of wisdom. The book of Proverbs describes the mouth that speaks these words as the "*mouth of the righteous*" or "*a fountain of life*" or "*a fountain of wisdom.*"[27] The same book speaks of the tongue in this way,

> *"The tongue of the wise brings healing."*

> *"The soothing tongue is a tree of life, ..."*

> *"The tongue of the righteous is choice silver."*

> *"The tongue of the wise adorns knowledge, ..."*

> *"The hearts of the wise make their mouths prudent,
> and their lips promote instruction."*

"Gracious words are a honeycomb, sweet to the soul and healing to the bones."

"Like apples of gold in settings of silver is a ruling rightly given."[28]

It is not surprising that Solomon declared,

"The tongue has the power of life ..."[29]

and that

"... truthful lips endure forever."[30]

The Apostle Paul urged,

"Let your conversation be always full of grace, seasoned with salt, ..."[31]

To the church at Corinth he said,

"For in him you have been enriched in every way – with all kinds of speech and with all knowledge ..."[32]

We are to be enriched by the communication of each other.

"Do not let any unwholesome talk come out of your mouths, but only what is helpful for building others up according to their needs, that it may benefit those who listen."[33]

He expresses the same intention using the words edifying and strengthening. We have the power to nurture, to invite each other to live. Let's design our speech to serve the needs of others.

IIIIIIIIIIIIIIIIIIIIIIIIIIIIIIIIIIIIIIIIIIIIIIIIIIIIIIIIIIIIIIIIIIIIIIIIIIIIIIIIIIIIIIIIIIIIII

Words – The Power of Healing and Growth.

IIIIIIIIIIIIIIIIIIIIIIIIIIIIIIIIIIIIIIIIIIIIIIIIIIIIIIIIIIIIIIIIIIIIIIIIIIIIIIIIIIIIIIIIIIIIII

The Power of Invitation

I grow or diminish in the presence of others. Their responses to me invite me to live or die. When affirmed, encouraged, comforted, or invited to live, I thrive. Nurturing words and actions enable us to thrive physically, mentally, and emotionally. Hope is fostered. We move toward accomplishment. The fire of hope is ignited. Our path forward is lit. We see beyond sorrow or pain. We are compelled toward a future.

When my gifts are encouraged to expression, I am motivated. In the presence of unconditional love, I bear blossoms and fruit. Yes, I am even rescued from my weariness, my apathy, my desire to give up, or my inclination to retreat. Life is kindled by a kind word. My fears can be comforted and the soul becomes quiet in acceptance.

Hope may be the greatest gift one can give another. Hope for today and tomorrow is essential and urgent. It is a gift we can give each other. When my hope is weak, your hope can strengthen me. Hitching to your hope will lead me to stay engaged in the face of my doubts. Sharing hope, we are stronger together. Hope and faith are closely related. Hope looks forward. Faith reaches for the unseen with assurance. Paul's great hymn to love links the two closely. Faith reaches into the unknown with expectation ignited by hope. Linked with love, hope and faith are powerful. Love is the invitation to live. Love lives the reality of faith and hope in the rigors of daily living. Together they invite us to leave the present circumstances and venture forward to create the future we desire. They take us beyond ourselves.

Hope is the heart experience that comes from the enlightenment of the Spirit of wisdom revealed by God in Christ. Paul saw this when he spoke of

> *"... the eyes of your heart may be enlightened in order that you may know the hope to which he has called you, ..."*[34]

Glenn Tinder writes, "I think of hope as a fabric each one of us must weave, and then fashion into a garment, good for wearing, like Joseph's coat."[35] A fragile dream may be nurtured by hope and another's faith in you. Like a tender plant, those expectations can be cultivated into growth and fruitfulness.

We have amazing power in the lives of others. Many have touched the web of my life, setting the web atremble for good and growth. Early in my life of ministry Dr. Morley Hall, Dr. John Armstrong, and Dr. Maurice Flint saw potential, fostered expectations, gave me hope, expressed faith in me, and nurtured with guidance. They enriched and empowered my limited expectations of myself igniting a vision that has carried me for decades. They gave me hope when I was doubtful. When this plant was drooping in doubt, they watered and nurtured me to hope.

Life Initiating Phrases

The power of words to invite others to live, I call life initiating phrases. I will list a few of them and you will be able to add others from you experience.

Life Initiating Phrases

• I agree!	• Let's start a new trend.
• That's a great idea, let's explore it!	• I know you can make it work.
• That's a helpful observation.	• Good for you for trying hard.
• I couldn't do it that well.	• I'm glad you brought that up.
• You are on the right track.	• We should explore your idea more.
• That's a winner!	• You hit the nail on the head!
• I have faith in you.	• You've started something worthwhile.
• See, you did it.	• That is the first step, let's continue.
• I appreciate what you have done.	• Thanks for your help.

"For the mouth speaks what the heart is full of."[36]

This takes us to a deeper level. We must go beyond the words to the affective dimensions of our lives. Our pattern of relationships, thinking toward others, and our attitudes and feelings that are the spring from which words flow. Words may be considered the symptoms that are evidence of underlying conditions of the heart. They are shaped into words by our minds and expressed with emotions, often without much involvement of the will. Intentions may be subtle.

The Patterns of the Heart

Behaviour patterns, verbal communication style, emotional expressiveness are all developed quite early in life. Children mimic the environment in which they are raised. Children yell because that is the style of communication they have learned. Sarcasm is learned. Combative style is acquired. Sensitivity is also developed as a response to witnessed behaviour. No doubt there are inborn factors that influence us in growing up in our social world. However, it is my conviction that most behaviour and our emotional expression is acquired through observation and learning.

No child sits in their highchair designing cognitively how they will speak, feel or think. They do not intentionally develop a relational plan for their lives. The self is constructed in the context of our relational environment rather than by intentional choices. We become locked into habits and these patterns are housed in the brain and the physiology of our being.

Freeing ourselves from the tyranny of childhood patterns or response is one of the tasks of adulthood. This requires reflection by nurturing minds and choices which may discard undesired patterns and practice of new patterns. We affirm what is desired and change what is ineffective or undesirable. However, it is not only our families that shape us. Siblings, birth order, culture, and educational experience play important roles. Friendships are important for social development. Later spouses, business associates and inter-cultural experience may change us significantly.

As we mature, we take more responsibility for our interactions. Choice is an exercise of the will. We can strengthen the will as declared by psychiatrist, Anthony Assogioli.[37] We have the freedom to change patterns and develop new ones. It requires intentionality, understanding, and determination. The desire to change and the practice of change reshapes us. The social environment we choose and help to create has major impact.

The old *Legend of the Rabbi* illustrates the point. I will give an abbreviated version of the story.

In an ancient kingdom, a monastery of Christian monks lived and served the local community. They responded to the poor and others in need. As the years passed, their numbers decreased. As they aged, they became less responsive to the needs and turned inward. People ceased consulting with the monks and only visited the beautiful grounds for picnics and the natural environment. The monks became unhappy, critical of each other, and increasingly their numbers dwindled.

The Abbot, though old and weary, was deeply concerned. Hearing of a wise, elderly Rabbi, who came to the area, he decided to visit. They spent the day together. The Abbot shared his grave concern. The Rabbi had no answer but as they departed, he said, "The Messiah is among you." The Abbot reported the saying to the monks, who pondered the saying wondering what the Rabbi could have meant by his strange comment.

One said concerning another, "He certainly could not have meant Brother Joseph as he has such a sharp tongue." Another said, "It could not be Brother Alphonse for he is so slow and Brother Regis is so absent-minded." Some wondered if it could be the old Abbot. Each examined himself and concluded the Messiah was surely not him.

However, in the off chance that it could be any one of them, they began to treat one another with greater respect, courtesy, and humor.

The community observed these changes. Some youth began to enquire and consult with the Monks. They were so impressed with the "love evident among the brothers" that engagement increased. Soon one and then a second and a third of the young men, inspired by the Monks behaviour to each other, joined the monastery. That renewed its vitality and ministry in the community.

When the brothers began to invite one another to live, the community saw the change. Looking beyond ourselves and treating each other with respect and love is always noticed. Seeing others as worthy, created in the image of God, and relating accordingly as a pattern of our hearts will have dramatic effect for good.

The Power of Gratitude

A special friend of mine recently published a valuable book on how to change the world with three sacred sayings: *Thank You. I'm Sorry. Tell me More.*[38] The essence of these three sayings expresses respect, gratitude, apology. These grow out of a grateful heart and genuine respect for others. Competitiveness is out; complementarity is in. Defensiveness is replaced with openness. Me is replaced with we. If we were to make these three statements our default response to others, we would all win.

We all grow in the presence of gratitude that flows from a sincere "thank you," which is an invitation to live. The thank offering played an important role in the Old Testament. Paul constantly expresses thanks to those whom he served. You may remember the story of Jesus being invited to supper by Simon.[39] While reclining at the table, Mary came and anointed Jesus' feet with a very expensive bottle of ointment. The wealthy man questioned, "Why this waste?" Jesus interpreted the expression of the woman as one of gratitude and love. The host had not even shown the respect of foot washing, but this woman was grateful for the grace of forgiveness. Gratitude doesn't require complete understanding, but a thankful heart.

The Art of Resuscitation

Resuscitation is the art of restoring consciousness, breathing and heartbeat. CPR is sometimes referred to as Mouth-to-Mouth Resuscitation. In this manner oxygen is kept flowing to the brain when a person is not able to do that themselves. I have experienced what it was to be like this.

While SCUBA diving in the Gulf of Mexico (fortunately at only 35 feet), I ran out of air. Trying to suck air out of a mouthpiece when no air is available in your tank is a bad situation. My training had taught me not to panic. I signaled my buddy. He immediately responded sharing his mouthpiece with me as we ascended. He caused me to breathe again without which I may not have survived. His sharing was an invitation to live.

Inviting others to live is like causing them to breathe again. There are several words translated comfort in the Scripture. Lamech named his son, Noah, saying,

"He will comfort us in the labor and painful toil ... "[40]

That kind of relief from stress and anxiety is like causing one to breathe again. The word *"comfort"* in the New Testament has the imagery in it of "coming along side" to assist or to carry a load. It might be illustrated by Paul's reference to Onesimus, a slave of Philemon. Paul says,

"If he has done you any wrong or owes you anything,
charge it to me. "[41]

Paul was prepared to bear the debt of Onesimus. Paul also speaks of fellow-workers

"... they refreshed my spirit and yours also. "[42]

He also spoke of *"strengthening"* each other and *"edifying"* others which all descriptors of what it means to invite others to live.

What a gift we are given! The opportunity to so impact others as to invite them to live, to grow, to mature, to succeed, and to flourish. We can do so with words spoken with gentleness, affirmation, and sensitivity. We must focus on the other's need rather than our own. The empathy required is sensitive to where the person is at as there are periods of growth. If we encourage growth at the right timing it will have profound effect on others.

Explore and Interact

1. It may be most helpful to make a list of individuals who have invited you to live. Identify what it was that specifically encouraged you.

2. Are you a member of a group that has been helpful to you in your growth?

3. What "life initiating phrases" would you like to build into your daily language.

TIMOTHY'S REFLECTION

I stood
Before a blank canvas
I'd been standing
Very long
My mind and it
Completed for void
Time passed
As did many
One stopped and said,
"It will be wonderful."
And I began
To paint.

CHAPTER FOUR: DESTROYING LIFE IN OTHERS

The art of inviting others to die is alive and well. No doubt you have been invited to die, at least figuratively. The invitation may be subtle, overt, intended, or accidental. The outcome is assured. When it happens, we may feel judged, put down, rejected, diminished, or devalued. Often it is words. Sometimes it is attitudes that our antenna picks up. Some are much more sensitive and more readily impacted by these invitations. We will look at this later. The experience will be different for each of us.

Response to Invitations to Die

These invitations set our web of life atremble. If it is a subtle invitation, we may wonder what created the feelings we are experiencing. The clue is our emotional response. It may take a while to cognitively understand what just happened. Emotions are immediate, perhaps not understood. I may say to myself,

"Wow, that hurt!"

"What was that all about?"

"I feel like I was just thrown overboard."

"What did I do? I feel like I was thrown under the bus!"

A vague sense of injustice, anxiety, bewilderment, or confusion may be the first response. We are suddenly alone, cut off, or disconnected. This may quickly give way to mental questioning which is seeking understanding. It may feel like someone has just planted a weed in my garden. If nurtured the weed may become invasive and choke out fruitful plants. It is important to understand the process. Invitations to die choke the soul, retard growth of healthy thoughts and creative expression. They exhaust the recipient. Permitted to grow, they consume the nutrients from healthy intentions.

Understanding takes time. Some jump immediately to self-blame which is not a good or helpful response. Be gentle if you have that tendency. There may be many other reasons. Often, invitations to die arise from a pool of anger in the other person, a previous hurt, a preoccupation with other concerns. It may be just a thoughtless comment. It could be from a habit of sarcasm. Of course, some people have an ingrained habit of being nasty, a habit of inviting others to die. Trying to analyze their problem won't solve yours. Seeking to understand the motives of others is usually unproductive.

There are a couple of things we can do. Slow down the process of seeking understanding. Don't let the "weed" take over your garden. Paul uses an interesting phrase about thinking,

> *"... we take captive every thought to make it*
> *obedient to Christ."*[43]

Just focus on the phrase "take captive every thought to make it obedient." Who is in control? Is it your emotions, your thoughts or you? Paul obviously thought we could exercise captivity over our thoughts. The implication is that neither our emotions or our thoughts should be in control, but rather in captivity to something higher. I think he assumed that our will representing our values, beliefs, and commitments should take control of emotions and thoughts. Emotions and thoughts, if not controlled, respond to desires which can lead us astray. Invasive weeds, regardless of where they come from, can destroy the fruitfulness of our garden.

Let me illustrate. One of the sad realities of our culture is the number of youths committing suicide each year. Frequently, this is a result of bullying, berating, or cyberbullying. It is estimated that from 20 % to 40 % of youth worldwide experience bullying. It may start with teasing, rejecting, isolating but often escalates. It has led to many taking their lives. The risk of suicide rises over 35% if there is not security in the family. Mobile phones have become an instrument of torture and a vehicle of abuse. It's easier to abuse remotely, but the pain is just as great. Anonymity emboldens those who invite others to die. It is sometimes mob behaviour. Rumination on negative thoughts reinforces the message. Motivations may not be clear but the outcome is devastating.

Sharpened Tongues and Drawn Swords

Some people have an instinct for zeroing in on saying things that will be hurtful to others. They have a flare for speaking words of criticism, discouragement, judgment, or ridicule. It is not always clear what motivates such comments. It is probably complicated. Less difficult if you are the recipient is knowing the effect on you and learning to respond in a healthy way. Again, there is insightful help in Scripture to respond to lying, deceitful, slanderous, deceptive, or harsh words. Think of the following references as a catalogue of invitations to die.

"With their mouths the godless destroy their neighbors, ..."[44]

"The words of the reckless pierce like swords, ..."[45]

"... a harsh word stirs up anger."[46]

"Their throats are open graves; their tongues practice deceit."[47]

"His mouth is full of lies and threats; trouble and evil are under his tongue."[48]

"Everyone lies to their neighbor; they flatter with their lips but harbor deception in their hearts."[49]

"My companion attacks his friends; he violates his covenant. His talk is smooth as butter, yet war is in his heart; his words are more soothing than oil, yet they are drawn swords."[50]

"See what they spew from their mouths – the words from their lips are sharp as swords, ..."[51]

"They sharpen their tongues like swords and aim cruel words like deadly arrows."[52]

"They shoot from ambush at the innocent; ..."[53]

"They make their tongues as sharp as a serpent's; the poison of vipers is on their lips."[54]

What a list! Human nature has not changed. These individuals are alive and well. This powerfully captures the experience. The tongue can be a very destructive instrument. The attitude back of this effect is disrespect, a passion for insult, a desire to destroy, and disable. Let's explore this a little deeper because these invitations do not come only from enemies.

Death by Friendly Fire

Sometimes in the tragedy of war we will hear of accidental deaths referred to as "death by friendly fire." It refers to soldiers caught in the crossfire and accidentally shot by allies. Sometimes in our relationships for lack of knowledge, understanding, or care, people are hurt by friends. What a tragedy. Sometimes it in a time of anger when control is lost. Perhaps you have had the experience where, after hurtful expression, you have wished you had bitten your tongue rather than have spoken.

The Old Testament man, Job, experienced "death by friendly fire." Job is an example of unjust suffering wherein he lost family and all his wealth. He was visited by friends who came to comfort him. They did comfort him in silent presence for seven days. However, after that they could not contain their critique. They did not intend to destroy his faith but eventually began to pour out volumes of accusation, criticism, and judgment.[55] When Job could take it no more, he said to Bildad, his friend,

> *"How long will you torment me and crush me with words?"*[56]

Crushed with words was an apt description of Job's experience. Bildad was being legalistic, accusatory, and evidenced little discernment to other options. His friends concluded that Job's suffering was punishment and clearly his fault. They had an inadequate theology of suffering. They were like the disciples of Jesus, who upon encountering a blind man asked,

> *"Who sinned, this man or his parents, that he was born blind?"*
> *Jesus replied, "Neither this man nor his parents sinned, ..."*[57]

Sometimes, even friends can invite us to die with unwarranted assumptions and judgments.

The Psalmist also had this experience.

> *"If an enemy were insulting me, I could endure it; if a foe were*
> *rising against me, I could hide. But it is you, a man like myself,*
> *my companion, my close friend, with whom I once enjoyed*
> *sweet fellowship at the house of God, as we walked about*
> *among the worshipers."*[58]

He wrote in another place,

> *"Even my close friend, someone I trusted, one who shared my*
> *bread, has turned against me."*[59]

Such betrayal may not always be intentional from friends, but it is always painful. To be invited to die by a friend is deeply hurtful and soul-destroying. This is not uncommon in spousal relationships where anger prompts harsh words that are destructive.

Sometime the words are like a steely fist in a velvet glove. Barbs or thorns that are hidden in downy softness and soothing tones lie in wait to injure with subtlety.

Anger can be expressed in soothing tones of deception, but the hurt is bitter. Devious hurt is like anthrax that appears innocent but when present in the atmosphere is deadly, though unseen. There may be no more painful way to be invited to die than by the words of a friend.

Early Life Invitations to Die

Neglect, shaming, or discouragement in early life is deadly for the long term. Mitch Albom, in his acclaimed book, *The Five People You Meet in Heaven,* makes this clear. "All parents damage their children. It cannot be helped. Youth, like pristine glass, absorbs the prints of its handlers. Some parents smudge, others crack, a few shatter childhoods into jagged little pieces, beyond repair. The damage done by Eddie's father was, at the beginning, the damage of neglect."[60]

Unfortunately, damage may begin early. A street youth shared her story with me. "I was happy there (i.e. in a foster home) until I was nine. That's when my foster parents told me I was not their child after all, and I became an inconvenience to them… In the last foster home, I was happy until another foster kid, a boy, began raping me for over four years. I ran away." She had lived on the street since. Abuse, extreme or mild, is an invitation to die whether from friendly fire or others.

Not everyone in families is nurtured. Some are neglected, shamed, or devalued in overt or subtle ways. While working with juvenile delinquents, many stories surfaced of youth invited to die in families. Abusive talk, unfair punishment, frequent put downs, displeasure in the child expressed or implied and shaming as a form of punishment were frequent in the lives of these youth. They often found acceptance by those involved in crime.

Failure to thrive in educational contexts is frequent. There may be many reasons. Children with undiagnosed limitations to learning fall between the cracks. Such was my personal experience. There was no way to address my inability to replicate sounds verbally received. A crowded one-room school was part of the problem as well as an overwhelmed teacher. Inability to learn, for whatever reason, leads to frustration, anger and acting out.

|||||||||||||||||||||||||||||||||||||||||||||||||||||||||||||||||||||||||||||||||||||||||||

Hurt from friends and family stings.

|||||||||||||||||||||||||||||||||||||||||||||||||||||||||||||||||||||||||||||||||||||||||||

Re-framing the experience through understanding will often work to wash away the pain. This usually does not come until later. Forgiveness of self and others is an important step in achieving understanding that is not possible for children. A story many years ago (the source lost) illustrates the point.

The Animals had a School

"Once upon a time, the animals had a school. They studied four subjects – running, climbing, flying, and swimming – for ease of administration – all the animals took all the subjects.

The duck was good at swimming, better than the teacher, in fact. He made a passing grade in running, excelled in flying but hopeless in climbing. So, they made him drop swimming to practice more climbing. Soon he became average in swimming. But average is okay, and nobody worried much about it – except the duck.

The eagle was considered a troublemaker. In his climbing class, he beat everybody to the top of the tree, but he had his own way of getting there, which was against the rules. He always had to stay after school and write, "Cheating is wrong!" five hundred times. This kept him from soring, which he loved. But schoolwork comes first.

The bear flunked because they said he was lazy, especially in winter. His best time was summer, but school was closed for holidays. Even during the few days, he was there, he was in trouble for throwing his weight around as a bully.

The penguin never went to school because he couldn't leave home, and they wouldn't start a school out where he lived.

The rabbit started at the top of the class in running, but he had a nervous breakdown because of so much make-up work in swimming.

The poor turtle who was very persistent in many activities, and excelled in swimming, was the poorest student in climbing. Unfortunately, he became the first casualty when he was stepped on by the horse.

All in all, it was a great school in humility. Few got to do what they were really good at but clearly came to understand their de-

ficiencies. No one felt good about themselves but did have opportunity to work on their weak subjects."

This is not to disparage teachers as I taught college for many years. I know the
limits teachers work under. I have been wonderfully encouraged by many great
teachers. However, understanding the experience from the perspective of the
learner is important. This need not be the end of the road. With understanding and
healing we can benefit, even from our experience of being invited to die. Henri
Nouwen makes this point well. He suggests that experiencing healing coupled
with faith can lead to our become wounded healers in helping others.[61]

A Culture of Negativity

It appears to me that we have moved toward a culture of negativity. The art of critique is well developed. It has benefited in developing and improving technology.
However, when applied to social relationships criticism usually has negative outcomes in reactivity, feeling put down, or responding with anger. It is less common
to see correction as a means to growth.

We have become a litigious society wherein people sue for very little reason.
Confrontation that is disparaging rather than helpful is very common. Entertainment has a strong focus on humor defined as putting the other person down. Many
family shows seem to consist of putting others down, creating humor at the ex-
pense of another. Politics is built around destroying the credibility of the opponent
rather than having a positive platform. We are trained to be critical more than to
be constructive.

The entertainment industry contributes to permeating our culture with a critical attitude. In much programing humor is accomplished through sarcasm, put-
downs, and taking advantage of others. The web fosters a freedom of expression
and criticism outside of the context of relationships. The impersonal nature of
electronic communication appears to free a critical attitude. It is my observation
that a negative outcome of the emphasis in our educational system on the development of a critical mind, which leads to much creativity, also fosters a critical
attitude that carries over into relationships. Superficiality in relationships of caring concern contributes to a critical culture.

Common Killer Phrases

Change is a possibility if we identify the problem. Only if I acknowledge my
actions of inviting others to die and the invitations of others can we choose to
change. I want to clearly identify the phrases by which we typically invite others

to die. You may be able to add others. When studying at University of Toronto, I mentioned that I saw many people inviting others to die by criticism to a professor. He said he made a hobby of collecting "killer phrases." An interesting hobby, I thought. So here is a list. You can check it out to see if you use any of these or if you would add others.

Killer Phrases that Destroy

• A swell idea, but….	• That's too modern for this group!
• What bubble head thought that up?	• Let's discuss that later, not now.
• That won't work, we tried it before!	• Why start anything new right now?
• You don't understand the problem.	• That's against policy that can't change!
• We've never done it that way!	• That's a ridiculous comment!
• It's not in the budget, forget it!	• You just don't get it, do you?
• There I go, messing up again!	• And you call yourself a good person?
• Nobody is ready for that yet.	• Why haven't you considered….
• Don't be ridiculous!	• That's a stupid idea, forget it!
• You must have been dreaming or high!	• That is not worth considering!
• And you call yourself a man!	• You are not a cook; you're an arsonist!
• You don't have the smarts to do that!	• Let's get practical, that won't work!

Another author calls these kind of comments "Poisonous Quotes" and has compiled them into a book.[62] If you wish to become a master at this devilish art you may want to look it up. It is not really a very encouraging read. Randy Alcorn observes that there are people of whom he says, "They seem to wear their displeasure as a badge of honor."[63] Displeasure has the same effect whether by words, attitudes, or actions. Often, such communication becomes a habit. They may represent anger, hurt, defensiveness, or maybe just a habit. If we focus on the impact, we may wish to change if we find ourselves using these phrases or attitudes.

The Impact of Negativity

The fruit of communication may be poisonous to the recipient. If we labeled people as toxic, we might know to avoid them. The wounds inflicted are profound and pervasive. They may range from suicide to hurt feelings. A medical doctor, Dr. Grant Mullen, observed, "I was surprised to discover that more people were suffering from emotional pain than from physical pain."[64] Typically, these wounds are on the inside affecting the mind, spirit, or the heart. However, these wounds impact identity, our sense of dignity, but also manifest in bodily illness.

When experienced early in life, they curb creativity and cripple one's ability to face the trials of life. Hope drowns in despair. Dreams are killed, smothered in the realism of parents or cynicism. Children quickly learn not to share, or maybe not to dream or imagine possibilities. Imagination is intended to bridge the now with the could be. It can free us from the fetters of the past and create new avenues to explore. The visualization of what could be should not be killed by cruel realities of the present. We may choke on the dry dust of legalism that was created for past situations which are history – not the reality of now or the possibilities of the future. Such invitations into our lives spread the virus of defeat and inadequacy through our systems. Indifference is deadly. Elie Weisel said, "The opposite of love, I have found, is not hate, but indifference."[65] Anger is a fear-inducing instrument used by parents to control children and intimidate others. It often creates a very unproductive cycle.[66]

Words are rarely neutral. Whether the vehicle is sarcasm, backbiting, gossip, accusation, put down, or the use of killer phrases, the outcome is devastating and long lasting. We may be pushed into stupidity, belligerence, frustration, depression, or rebellion. We are affected physically, emotionally, spiritually, and relationally. Also, we take our failed selves into future relationships and often spread the poison.

IIIIIIIIIIIIIIIIIIIIIIIIIIIIIIIIIIIIIIIIIIIIIIIIIIIIIIIIIIIIIIIIIIIIIIIIIIIIIIIIIIIIIIIIIIII

Killer phrases are toxic.

IIIIIIIIIIIIIIIIIIIIIIIIIIIIIIIIIIIIIIIIIIIIIIIIIIIIIIIIIIIIIIIIIIIIIIIIIIIIIIIIIIIIIIIIIIII

A Biblical illustration will make the point. Israel was in slavery in Egypt for several decades. They came to accept their role and so defined their identity. When God rescued them with the leadership of Moses, they traveled to the border of the promised land. They sent spies into the land to survey the situation. They found abundance and fruitfulness. However, the people seemed large and powerful. Joshua and Caleb want to go into the land. The others gave a "bad report" saying the occupants were giants. Their comment,

> *"We seemed like grasshoppers in our own eyes, and we looked the same to them."*[67]

This view of themselves may have had more to do with the fact that they had not freed themselves from their identity as slaves than it had to do with the enemy they faced. Our perception of ourselves, as shaped by the response of others, has dramatic effect. They turned away from the Promised land as defeated before the battle even started. The outcome of invitations to die destroys identity and hope.

Explore and Interact

1. Have you experienced "death by friendly fire?" Explore, without judgment, the phrases that impacted you. What values or expectations were challenged? Write down how it felt. Writing helps to make it objective so you can evaluate the issues.

2. Can you identify any shaming, negative comparisons, or put-downs you experienced as a young person? Writing about it may bring freedom and objectivity.

3. Can you identify your own favorite phrases that may have toxicity for others? Acknowledging these may give you the freedom to break the habit.

TIMOTHY'S REFLECTION

Jane's doll's head came off
Jane gasped in horror
Her doll's head came off
And she was horrified
Jane found some tape
Green tape of her father's
And began winding it around
And around the neck
Of the injured doll.
She held the doll's neck in place
While she taped it
With the tape she found
That her Dad had.
When her father saw her, he gasped
"What have you done?"
She held up the doll.
"Why, you saved her life
What a great little doctor you are!"
She became a great doctor
Saving many lives.
Jane's dad came to her,
"Oh, you broke your doll
You used up the last of my tape.
Don't do stuff like that!"
She never practiced science again
And saved no one.
She was just Jane.

CHAPTER FIVE: A PLACE FOR GROWTH

Growth is a sign of life. Most people want to encourage others to growth, accomplishment, and to fulfillment. That's inviting others to live! What achieves this in others? What fosters creativity? If you aim at nothing, you hit it every time. How do we become intentional, good at inviting others to live? If we do so, negativity will drop on the wayside. If we invite others to live, we set their life web atremble for all kinds of good things to happen.

What to Do and Not Do

Focusing our goal and clarifying our intention is the place to start. Goals need to be definable, believable, achievable, measurable, and stated with no alternative. The best way to make them definable is to write them down. Believable means that must be consistent with our values. Achievable indicates they must be within our abilities (with the help of others). Our progress must be measurable stated in steps which is a very motivating factor. Stated with no alternative means they are more than wishes. They are commitments. Commitments are made up front. If we clarify our commitments before the test of circumstances, we are less likely to be distracted by challenges.

IIIIIIIIIIIIIIIIIIIIIIIIIIIIIIIIIIIIIIIIIIIIIIIIIIIIIIIIIIIIIIIIIIIIIIIIIIIIIIIIIIIIIIIIIIII

Clarify commitment before circumstances.
Thwart intention.

IIIIIIIIIIIIIIIIIIIIIIIIIIIIIIIIIIIIIIIIIIIIIIIIIIIIIIIIIIIIIIIIIIIIIIIIIIIIIIIIIIIIIIIIIIII

The other side of the coin from what to do clarifies what not to do. Wishes are rooted in desires and change with the wind of emotions. Commitments are an expression of the will and are as solid as our values. Values clarified provide the foundation for life. Don't wish, commit! Most of the time analyzing the past is a waste of time unless you are well trained in that area. Simply regurgitating the past keeps you stuck in history. We are seeking to create the future we want. We want it to be different than the past. Guidance can help us learn from the past, but clarifying the future is of necessity in the end.

The New Testament is primarily about the future lived in love, hope, and faith. Yes, Jesus deals with our past and made forgiveness possible but he wants us to create the future he desires. He was clear about the function of the community he came to create and the future he wanted us to anticipate.

Creating a Growth Environment

Every living thing is designed for growth. Three things are required to assure growth. You need good seed and a good environment to begin with. Even good seed will not grow in a poor environment. I discovered that in trying to grow grass. Jesus described the effect of seed when it falls in a poor environment such as hard or stony ground.[68] The environment must be prepared. The potential for life is in the seed. The environment is the context for growth. Life in the seed provides the potential for growth, the environment, the context. The planter does not create the miracle of life but can do much to facilitate it.

If the seed is good and the prepared environment is provided the caregiver can provide much impact on what happens. Enabling growth to excel is in the power of the caregiver. We, then, have the power to affect growth through the dynamics of nurture. Applying this analogy, we can understand our power to invite others to live or die. This is suggested by Jesus in the parable following that of the Sower. He speaks of the impact of weeds. Weeds seem to appear naturally but, as Jesus suggested, it could be the work of the enemy.

The dynamic of nurture includes applying fertilizer, water, adequate sunshine, shade, and all the nutrients necessary. Plants only produce maximum growth with needed care. They need protection and nurture. It is so with people also. Children grow or thrive with protection and nurture. This is also the case with adults. We can provide the environment, protection, and nurture that we each need for growth. We never outgrow our need for each other to serve this function in our relationships. People wither, shrivel, experience defeat or depression, and withdraw from life and creativity without nurture in an environment conducive to growth. This is our gift to each other.

Our bodies are like that. If one part of the body is not functioning well, many other functions will be affected. Infection spreads through the body. Pain in one part impacts other parts. When I had two knee replacements, I discovered this to be true. A friend who had a knee replaced began to limp and destroyed a hip. The parts are mysteriously integrated and require health in each other to function in harmony.

||||||||||||||||||||||||||||||||||||||||||||||||||||||||||||||||||||||||||||||||||||||||||||||
Commit to create community.
||||||||||||||||||||||||||||||||||||||||||||||||||||||||||||||||||||||||||||||||||||||||||||||

That is also true of our relational community. One abrasive person in a group can affect the whole group. Mob behaviour is certainly an example of that. People in mobs do things they would not do alone and often regret mob behaviour. Just like toxicity spreads through our physical bodies it may spread through a group. Evil can thrive and compete with good nurturing.

The Will to Nurture

We don't nurture plants unless we have the will to do so. As a child I was expected to hoe the garden, to weed, and to water the plants. I often did so unwillingly. My mother's favorite house plant was the gloxinia. She had five colors. She nurtured them relentlessly. They had priority. They bloomed profusely. She constantly re-planted them to larger containers, better environments. They never lacked for love or nutrients. She was committed to those flowers with a strength of will and determination.

We must have a will to nurture others. Motivation is a function of will. In our Western culture, we have come to place a great stress on freedom of choice, es-pecially personally defined. This is often determined by personal desires. Desires activate emotions and they give rise to desire. They are closely related but differ-ent. Emotions are indicative of the meaning of something to the person. Desires will seek to use or change the situation to achieve an outcome we wish, often to achieve the emotion we enjoy. Emotions and desires are not the best guide to our behaviour.

The will is value driven. The beliefs or values to which we are committed are more stable and enduring. The analogy of a ship may help. It you guide your ship by the stars you will have a stable course to your destination. If you guide your ship by the clouds, you will be tossed to and fro as the clouds respond to the wind, The will directed by values is more like the stars in stability. If we clarify our commitments with our values before we encounter challenging situations, we are more likely to be consistent than if we guide our decisions by shifting desires or emotions.

Many examples clarify this principle. In Gethsemane, Jesus prayed, "My Father, if it is possible, may this cup be taken from me. Yet not as I will, but as you will." He submitted his desire to the higher purpose of his Father.[69] Daniel and his three friends when in captivity determined not to breach their values. When faced with the option of the fiery furnace they remained consistent to their commitment rather than responding to the fearful prospects of the furnace.[70] They had clarified their commitment prior to the test of circumstances. We are much more likely to invite others to live if we clarify a commitment to do so. That commitment enables us to plan the how that we will use to accomplish our intent.

|||||||||||||||||||||||||||||||||||||||||||||||||||||||||||||||||||||||||||||||||||||||||

Commit to intent; accomplish in action.

|||||||||||||||||||||||||||||||||||||||||||||||||||||||||||||||||||||||||||||||||||||||||

From a Christian point of view, we must acknowledge our need for the grace of God to enable our choice and commitment. The enablement to function beyond our own interests is the work of the Holy Spirit within. My brother-in-law, Pastor Reid Cooke puts it this way, "God has made a way for us. It is called grace. It is what God does within us, without us."[71] To experience this grace, we need the salvation and enabling of the Spirit that God provides in Jesus. Paul, the apostle knew this.

> *"For what I want to do I do not do, but what I hate I do. ... For I have the desire to do what is good, but I cannot carry it out."*[72]

He, then, adds that the war within self can be carried out,

> *"... through Jesus Christ our Lord!"*[73]

Spiritual enablement, beyond ourselves, is available in Christ.

Creating the Community for Growth

Growth in relationships happens in a community with others. A community is a group of people who associate around things they have in common. It may be social, religious, occupational, professional, or any other interest. They share. In the plant world it may refer to a group of plants sharing the same environment. Sharing is the central idea. Humans are designed to share. Neurologically, we even replicate the emotions of those around us. We are just not created to be loners.

Think back to Adam and Eve and creation. The only thing not good about creation was that Adam was alone. God said,

> *"It is not good for the man to be alone."*[74]

But, didn't man have perfect fellowship with God? That was not enough, he needed someone like himself. Eve was to be his partner. Later, God chose a community, Israel, to be his people. He gave them many instructions about morality, caring for creation, and relating to himself. However, much of his instruction was directed to their relationships with each other. Community was central to their being.

Community provides the context for growth. Hillary Clinton made that claim in her book, *It Takes a Village*.[75] Not only a village but a family is required. If the family and village are one in values and commitments, you have a winning combination. God works through communities. The examples are Israel and the churches of the New Testament wherein they cared for each other. A person may come to faith alone, but no one can survive in the life of faith alone.

||||||||||||||||||||||||||||||||||||||||||||||||||||||||||||||||||||||||||||||||||||||||||||||||

Fulfillment in living requires community.

||||||||||||||||||||||||||||||||||||||||||||||||||||||||||||||||||||||||||||||||||||||||||||||||

Many argue that "the old forms of community have unraveled" and with this loss "people have lost the sense of inclusion and belonging... The community stagnates without the impulse of the individual. The impulse dies away without the sympathy of the community."[76] We are born into relationships within the family. We thrive in relationships within community. Harmony between the individual and the community maximizes potential for both. Peter Alishire sums it up, "The need for contact, communication and compassion have been programmed into the functioning of the cells of our immune system, the walls of our coronary arteries, and our very will to live.[77] Hermon Melville is quoted as saying, "We cannot live for ourselves. Our lives are connected by a thousand invisible threads, and along these sympathetic fibers, our actions run as causes and return to us as results."[78] Walter C. Averez (Associate at the Mayo Clinic) asserted that happiness and health may be related to the appreciative responses from others.[79]

The power enabling us to rise above self to care for others is a focus of the New Testament community through the dynamic of agape love. This is the unique love, enabled by the Holy Spirit of God as we unite in grace with Christ. Community is essential for well-being. We thrive in relationships that nurture us. We must move beyond self to incorporate others into our web of life.

Moving from Me to We

Seeking harmony, mutual support, between self and others is essential to the fulfillment of each of us as individuals. Most agree that in the Western world we have moved to a strong individualism that focus on personal rights, self-fulfillment, or what is called atomism by Charles Taylor, quoted earlier. We cannot fulfill oneself without others. We need to move from me to we. "We cannot find reality simply by remaining within ourselves or making ourselves the goal. Paradoxically, we only know ourselves when we know ourselves responding to others."[80] Graces toward oneself is a necessary condition for the experience of grace toward others. Grace enables acceptance which opens the pathway to change. We must move toward a place where community fulfills the individual and the individual completes community.

Belonging is the humus, the earthly medium, for nurturing human growth. Humus is essential for the fertility of the soil. Interestingly, humus is created by dying vegetable matter. Jesus taught that death to self by putting others ahead of self leads to both growth for self and others. This is moving from me to we. The community creates safety for the individual to experience, value, honor, acceptances, nurture, and love. The individual in turn nurtures his neighbours to life and growth. The Apostle Paul declares that it doesn't work when

"For everyone looks out for their own interests, not those of Jesus Christ."[81]

but recommends that

"Carry each other's burdens, and in this way you will fulfill the law of Christ."[82]

and that

"Each of us should please our neighbors for their good, to build them up."[83]

||||||||||||||||||||||||||||||||||||||||||||||||||||||||||||||||||||||||||||||||||||||||||||

Community is no accident; it is intentional.

||||||||||||||||||||||||||||||||||||||||||||||||||||||||||||||||||||||||||||||||||||||||||||

Community is like a jigsaw puzzle. A piece alone is not much. Each peace is shaped slightly differently. The picture is not complete until every piece is in place. This is a picture of community and of moving from me to we. We are each different. We are complimentary. We cannot say of another piece,

"I have no need of you."[84]

We are all needed and have a role to play. For a period, I worked in a psychiatric hospital. It was unique as a therapeutic community. The uniqueness was in that every person, including the patients, were expected to care for each other in very clearly defined ways. This expectation created the care in the community, not just the professionals who provided treatment according to their skills. Everyone contributed to everyone else. This was the intention of Jesus for his community, the church. Moving from me to we has the potential of realizing his intention. We nurture each other by inviting each other to live.

Explore and Interact

1. Identify what creates a "growth environment" for you personally. What do you find affirming and encouraging? What is nurturing for you?

2. How would you rate your pursuit of individualistic goals as compared to your concern for others and their needs on a ten point scale?

3. Would you find it difficult to move from me to we? Do you know how others can best strengthen you and you them? List the ways.

TIMOTHY'S REFLECTION

I looked unbiased
Upon my words
I watched them leave my mouth
They were irretrievable and potent
They could dance and weave
Dart and plummet.
They cast spells of no intent
Or lay baking and waiting.
Some of them drew upon each other
And seemed large
Just by their own interpretation.
Some were projectiles
Weapons of destruction.
A pathetic few
Were powerful, kind
And full of potential strength
Very many
Were at best
Warm air.
I vowed to silence
To hold my tongue
Since it had little value to offer
But nothing
Would come out
And when it did
The silence
Was often useless
And misplaced.
I pondered my state
And instead
Decided to communicate
With decisiveness
Care
And empathy.

CHAPTER SIX: THE TAPESTRY OF CHRISTIAN ENGAGEMENT

Perspective is the key. Seeing the Grand Canyon from 30,000 feet is quite different from seeing it while rafting down the Colorado River. We have used analogies of the spider's web, gardening, the function of the body, and death by friendly fire. We could also look at it from the perspective of citizenship. Another view would be from the perspective that Christ and the Apostles presented in the New Testament. I would like to combine the idea of citizenship and the view of the New Testament into the imagery of a tapestry. They fit well together.

The Tapestry of Participation in the Fellowship of Faith

A tapestry is created in many ways which often involves bringing different colored threads together in creating the artistic image the creator has in mind. A poet may choose to use words to create his masterpiece. It is interesting that Paul, the apostle, speaks of the community of faith as God's masterpiece[85] which in some translations is rendered, "workmanship." This is the word from which we get our English word "poem." The word is much broader than our understanding of poetry. It really means "the work of one's hands" and references all creative expression. It is assumed that creativity reveals the person who expresses the creativity.

The fellowship of faith, what we refer to as the church, is intended to demonstrate the work of God in the lives, individually and in community, of those who choose to commit to him. Let me develop that a little. When a person chooses to commit to God, he/she becomes indwelt by the Holy Spirit of God. Henceforth they are expected to manifest the life of Christ in their lives. Paul prayed,

> *"For this reason I kneel before the Father, from whom every*
> *family in heaven and on earth derives its name. I pray that*
> *out of his glorious riches he may strengthen you with power*
> *through his Spirit in your inner being, so that Christ may dwell*
> *in your hearts through faith. And I pray that you, being rooted*
> *and established in love, may have power, together with all the*
> *Lord's holy people, to grasp how wide and long and high and*

> *deep is the love of Christ, and to know this love that surpasses*
> *knowledge – that you may be filled to the measure of all the*
> *fullness of God. ... I urge you to live a life worthy of the calling*
> *you have received."*[86]

I am mixing my metaphors of tapestry and building. Jesus used the metaphor of building when he declared, "I will build my church." Paul speaks of the relationships of believers in such a way as it lends itself more to the image of weaving a tapestry. Paul's focus is on the relational nature of the church. Having experienced a relationship with God through faith in Christ requires manifestation in living relationships in this fellowship of faith. This necessitates a focus on the dynamics of encounter with each other in the context of our vast differences. From his perspective there is no dimension of our existence that supersedes our relational responsibility to each other, apart from the foundational and personal relationship with have with God. This means that gender, race, language, or all the other things that differentiate us are of less importance than our engagement with each other. He develops a new descriptive language to describe these relationships.

The strength of a tapestry is dependent upon the strength of the cords. However, when woven together the strength is multiplied by the combining in the weaving of the cords to each other. The outcome is a multiplication of strength. We are stronger together is more than a political catch phrase; it is a literal truth. We need clarity concerning the relational aspects that strengthen us

Tapestries are strong because of the weaving of threads, weak in themselves, but strengthened by being woven together. Our strength is greater together. We contribute to each other. We are together one body, a unit, combined by God to serve in equal concern for one another.[87] The strength of the community of faith, the church, is known through this dynamic citizenship which binds all believers together.

The Creation of a Culture of Commitment

Cultures in our world are distinguished by many variables such as language, dress, habits of expression, common origins, and other distinctions. We each become expressions of the culture in which we are raised and nurtured. I continue decades later to manifest some of the qualities of the culture of frugality created by world wars and the depression of the early twentieth century. If we become part of the culture created by our relationship with Christ, we will demonstrate qualities, behaviour, the different lifestyle that is characteristic of that culture. In the Old Testament, God called Israel to be his people that they might be a witness to the nations who did not know God. He gave them detailed instruction how they were to live in relation to each other, demonstrating to the nations the difference that relationship to him made. Paul declares,

> *"... if anyone is in Christ, the new creation has come: The old has gone, the new is here!"*[88]

Jesus urged people,

> *"But seek first his kingdom and his righteousness, ..."*[89]

Paul spoke of our citizenship being in heaven. The community of faith is to manifest the qualities of living evidencing where our citizenship resides.

The commonality sought in the culture of a Christian community is spiritual. It is not conformity in clothing, common origins, physical features, or other surface differences. It grows from a common commitment in faith to Jesus Christ, his values, and his commitment to obedience to the Father. It requires a commitment to values. What God desires of us is revealed in the Scripture. The Word of God provides the manual for belief and behaviour. Paul has much to say about the enablement that comes through the indwelling of God's Spirit in the believer.

> *"I keep asking that the God of our Lord Jesus Christ, the glorious Father, may give you the Spirit of wisdom and revelation, so that you may know him better. I pray that the eyes of your heart may be enlightened in order that you may know the hope to which he has called you, the riches of his glorious inheritance in his holy people, and his incomparably great power for us who believe."*[90]

The achievement of citizenship is through birth into Christ's kingdom through faith.

The benefits of citizenship are many. Paul gives a partial list as he writes to the church at Philippi,

> *"... encouragement from being united with Christ, if any comfort from his love, ... common sharing in the Spirit, ... tenderness and compassion, ... not looking to your own interests but each of you to the interests of the others. ... have the same mindset as Christ Jesus: ... for it is God who works in you ..."*[91]

This is a partial list. The benefits come from a new relationship with God the Father and from the relationship with fellow citizens in the household of faith.

The qualities of relationship among those who have this citizenship is clearly identified.

The Tapestry of Relationships

The key to health in relationships is the behaviour of love. The word for love in the New Testament is unique in the language of the world of early Christianity. It is a different word than that used to describe erotic love, family love or friendship love. It arises from the work of God's Spirit in the life of the believer and has its foundation in the will rather than emotions, familial or friendship relationships. It is motivated toward the needs of the recipient. It is responsive to the other rather than arising as a desire or need in the giver. The motivation is God's love and

> *"God's love has been poured out into our hearts through the Holy Spirit, who has been given to us."*[92]

> *"This is how we know what love is: Jesus Christ laid down his life for us. And we ought to lay down our lives for our brothers and sisters."*[93]

This dynamic of love, as we conform to it, leads us to reach beyond self to a deep concern for each other and even to embrace our enemies. This love is extreme. Jesus said,

> *"You have heard that it was said, 'Love your neighbor and hate your enemy.' But I tell you, love your enemies and pray for those who persecute you, ..."*[94]

He further illustrated this with the story of the Good Samaritan who cared for the person robbed, beaten, and left on the side of the road. This dynamic certain takes us beyond ourselves.

The Tapestry of Behaviour

The dynamic of love is illustrated by the behaviour in relationships. It is more than emotion. It involves action at the level of real, down-to-earth needs. Our entire lives speak into each relationship we enter. It is both our behaviour and our conversation that are important. Each of these are expressions of our attitudes, values, and emotions. behaviour and conversation are shaped from the inside out. It is our inner being, sometimes referred to as our heart, that directs both our speech and our behaviour. This is clearly the burden of the New Testament whether we look at the life of Christ or the teaching of the Apostles. Let's look at each of these briefly in summary as we have touched on these earlier in this book.

We have indicated the importance of the inner aspects of attitudes, our affective responses, and the role of our wills. The words of the New Testament that bring these into focus are love, grace, patience, kindness, goodness, longsuffering, attitudes of peace, joy, and self-control. Many of these are identified as the fruit of the Spirit of God in our lives. Paul says,

"Against such things there is no law."[95]

Love is presented as supreme. However, this is a special kind of love, differentiating it from erotic love, family love, or friendship love as noted above. This love is an act of will rather than a response of emotion and is enabled by our relationship with God through faith. Attitudes are expressed in the terms of humility, compassion, tenderness, and the capacity to seek the interest of others instead of our own.

Verbs are the action aspects of our expression of ourselves in behaviour. Both attitudes and emotions are given wheels by the behaviour we demonstrate in relationships. There is overlap between attitudes, emotions, and behaviour. In many ways the behaviour is an extension of these attitudes. For example, the behaviour of forgiveness is powerfully motivated by humility, compassion, tenderness, and love. Some of the most important action words in the New Testament describing the desired behaviour in the tapestry of Christian community are fellowship, edification, comfort, encouragement, like-mindedness, being slow to anger, putting the interests of others ahead of self, and strengthening one another. These are all behaviours of the love that is the foundation of our relationships.

A few of these words are not common in our usage. The word "*fellowship*" essentially means the making of my resources available to another to respond to their needs. Seeking "*like-mindedness*" does not mean giving up my own mind but rather seeking a common mind with others rather than focusing on differences. "*Comfort*" in Paul's language contains the picture of coming alongside of another person to help them lift their load or burden. Since these words are frequently found in Scripture, I will not list all the references. However, your reading of the New Testament will enable you to identify them in their context. Thus, the graphics would look like this.

From Convictions to Attitudes to Bahaviours

→	→	→
• Belief	• Patience	• Fellowship
• Value	• Kindness	• Edification
• Will	• Goodness	• Comfort
• Attitudes	• Compassion	• Encouragement
• Emotions	• Longsuffering	• Interests of others
	• Tenderness	• Strengthening others

Speech is one of the outcomes of this equation. These are the attitudes, values, emotions that provide the spring from which should flow our speech in conversation. We discussed the dimensions of communication in chapter two. When you add speech that is designed to invite people to live to the equation above, you have a powerful impact on people. When speech is an outcome of these, it is easy to understand where the power comes from. It is also clear as to why we need the transformation which relationship with God brings to enable communication designed to invite people to live. Our communication is powerful and comes from the depths of our being.

When we understand the power of speech and its impact on others arises from deep places in our being it becomes clear why Paul places a strong emphasis on the need to

"... be transformed by the renewing of your mind."[96]

Also, we can understand why James, the brother of Jesus, urged each of us to

"... keep a tight rein on their tongues ..."[97]

and to

"... keep the royal law found in Scripture, 'Love your neighbor as yourself, ...'"[98]

These are closely related.

These are the threads that are woven into the tapestry of Christian community as in God's grace we create the culture of love. The community of faith is God's creation as he calls individuals into relationships of love and service. By his transforming grace the citizenship of heaven can be begin to be practiced, however incompletely, in our relationships as we invite each other to live.

Explore and Interact

1. The place to begin is to explore and fulfill our relationship with God. That is the foundation. They we can seek, by grace, to work on bring our values, attitudes, behaviours, and speech into line with our will to invite others to live.

2. A helpful exercise would be put this chapter in your own words and explore how it could apply to your life in specific and actual relationships. This may be in your family, your work, or your social context.

3. How could you begin to work on your life patterns?

TIMOTHY'S REFLECTIONS

I dreamed of a great yet odd gift.
It was a small round marble.
With omnipotent perspective
I gazed the maze
That was my life.
Viewing of the path the ball took
Was less than spectacular
In its confines.
Disappointment –
Expectation was
To see the fruits of my labour
And to celebrate
The rights of freedom
My choices allowed,
Yet the walls I built
Were constricting,
Embarrassingly predictable,
With an obvious and naïve intention
For self-betterment
That was failing colossally.
Even my future
Was stiff and constricted
With poor decisions
Supported by the ramparts
I would build.
To my right
Was the true maze builder.
One whom I'd never seen
Or thought to yield employment.
The builder had a beatific aura.
I offered my future and all of me
For the builder's direction.
Looking back to
My labyrinth of life
All my perspective walls had fallen.
My future was an open, blank book
Of possibilities and wonder
With interwoven access
To all of those around me
For whom I felt new love
Compassion and duty.

We could make us much better
With its guidance.
The thrill of a child
Filled my heart
And spirit.

CHAPTER SEVEN: THE ART OF NAVIGATING RELATIONSHIPS

Our relationships have a powerful impact. The impact is reciprocal. It is a two-way street. We affect others and they affect us. There are many parts to this influence. Our values and attitudes shape our expressions. They manifest in physical ways including body posture, gestures, and our eyes. Indeed we speak with our bodies. That which is inside of us leaks out, usually unconsciously, in a multitude of ways. Words and behaviour are outward expression of all that we are as persons. We may seek to cover up with acting, intentionally distorting, deceiving intentionally what we know to be our true feelings. This, in the long run becomes self-defeating. Acting may be entertaining on the stage, but it is devastating in real life. It will destroy rather than build relationships.

Exploring the Art

All artistic endeavors require the creative bringing together of many elements. A painting requires the instruments, such as brush, paint, canvas, etc. But requires the imaginative conception of the artist and her commitment to the project with the required skill to execute her vision necessary for completion. What is within the painter must come to expression. Many artists benefit greatly from teachers and colleagues who provide affirmation and encouragement. Navigating requires many contributing factors to be successful.

We have defined the art of navigating relationships as needing attention to many elements. In our person we bring values, beliefs, attitudes, motivations and all the dimensions of our emotional and spiritual beings. We acquire expressive, physical aspects of communication such as gesture, body language and the habit of looking others in the eye (or not) which dramatically impact our relationships. The verbal skills we develop, including the extensiveness of our language acquisition, contributes. The art of navigating relationships is as complicated as any other creative or skilled production. A carpenter is dependent upon the quality of his tools. A lawyer is dependent upon his knowledge of law as well as his skills as a communicator.

The skills of relationship functioning do not come naturally. They need to be acquired and developed in much the same ways as skills in expressive art, building, or landscaping. Very few people have the skills of piano playing without much practice. The person constructing a house requires many skills and much knowledge.

In relationships, we must be intentional to seek the development of relational skills that will express our desires and emotions to accomplish the purposes desired. Think for a moment about the skills required to comfort someone who has been bereaved. If we have not developed the skills, we will feel awkward as will the person we are seeking to comfort. In reality, we require both expressive and receptive abilities to function well in relationships. Earlier, we identified the skills necessary to function in the New Testament community. Those same skills will help us to be effective in all relationships. The acquisition of skills will happen only if we intentionally seek to develop them.

In my extensive work in other cultures and with people serving as doctors, nurses, educators, and missionaries, it was clear that specific attitudes and clear intentions were needed for successful function in those other cultures. Certainly, language acquisition required a set of skills, often achieved over extended time. We need to put equal effort into learning how to invite others to live.

It may be helpful if I provide some definitions that set Paul's expectations apart from the usual meaning of the word above as they are used today. The problem is in the translation. For example, the word "fellowship" in the New Testament has very specific meaning and begins to be used in the early days of the church. Its common usage had to do with money. In the Epistles the word is translated "contribution," as in financial contribution to those in need. An appropriate definition would be: using our personal resources in generosity to meet the needs of another person or organization. The assumption is that my resources, whether personal gifts or money, are a gift from God and it is my responsibility to share these with others as they share theirs with me. It is a reciprocal experience.

The word definition is a word of construction which essentially means constructing or building something to completion. "Comfort" is often a very strong word which contains in it the idea of an enduring support that brings assistance to another. The basic idea in comfort is to come along side of another to assist in lifting their burden. "Encouragement" is also a strong word expressing affirmation. A strong emphasis in the New Testament was that the members of the fellowship were to be preoccupied with meeting the needs of each other in every way possible. The concern for others was to supersede one's own needs, or at least to be considered equal. This is illustrated in Barnabas selling his property to meet the needs of others. There was a very strong emphasis on communal responsibilities in the early church. As we have seen, the concept of love is unique to the New Testament in that there is no real illustration in secular literature that employs the term "agape" as it is used in the New Testament.

Incarnating the Art

Perhaps the best way to illustrate the incarnation of the art is to go to an illustration in Scripture.

God created humans in his own likeness in ways we do not fully understand. It is obvious that he intended to have fellowship, that is relationship, with man. This intention was aborted by the schemes of Satan. Man chose to obey Satan rather than God. A tragic separation occurred. Immediately, God began a plan to redeem the situation, to achieve his goal of communion with man. He befriended Abraham. He walked with Enoch. He wanted more than individual relationships and chose the slaves in Egypt to become his people. To enable the transition from slavery to a people of God, it was necessary for him to reveal himself. He did so in graciously providing for them, not just in rescuing them from Egypt, but providing for them through the wilderness wanderings and into a Promised Land. They didn't respond well.

God, over generations, sent prophets to communicate his grace and desire for relationship. In reality, it seemed ineffective in accomplishing his purpose. The writer of the New Testament book of Hebrews expresses it this way:

> *"In the past God spoke to our ancestors through the prophets at many times and in various ways, but in these last days he has spoken to us by his Son, ..."*[99]

The life of Jesus was God the Father speaking to us. The life of Jesus was the voice of God. In his incarnation he became

> *"... just as we are – yet he did not sin."*[100]

The life of Jesus becomes an example for us. He demonstrated the Father in his behaviour and speech which was an expression of his character.

In the same way, our behaviour and speech are the incarnation, that is the expression, of who we are in values, beliefs, commitments, and attitudes. Often, it is our verbal expression that is the first impression people get of us. This enables us to grasp the reason that our words are so powerful. If they express an invitation to live or to die, they are often the front line in people getting to know who we are. Thus, we must be careful that they represent what we really want them to represent. Their expression may be uplifting or devastating. The words, of course, are enhanced by the non-verbal aspects of communication in our body language. Much body language is controlled by the autonomic part of our nervous system and may more accurately represent us than the words over which we have conscious control. Words may be used deceptively. Non-verbal expressions are less likely to be deceptive because they tend to be automatically expressed.

||||||||||||||||||||||||||||||||||||||||||||||||||||||||||||||||||||||||||||||||||||

Clarify; develop the skills;
incarnate the behaviour.

||||||||||||||||||||||||||||||||||||||||||||||||||||||||||||||||||||||||||||||||||||

The Complexity of the Art of Relating

Navigating relationships is complex. This complexity is a central theme of the Biblical story. It goes back to the story of the Garden of Eden. The relationship between Adam and Eve began with their encouragement to disobey God by Satan. Their relationship was lost. Adam blamed Eve:

> *"The woman you put here with me – she gave me some fruit*
> *from the tree, and I ate it."*

The woman, when confronted said,

> *"The serpent deceived me, and I ate."*[101]

This beginning is the continued story through the history of mankind. All human relating to others became driven by self-interest and desires. This was summed up in the words,

> *"... everyone did as they saw fit."*[102]

Or, to express it another way,

> *"In their own eyes they flatter themselves too much to detect*
> *or hate their sin. The words of their mouths are wicked and*
> *deceitful; ..."*[103]

The same theme is acknowledged in the New Testament.

"I do not understand what I do. For what I want to do I do not do, but what I hate I do. And if I do what I do not want to do, ... it is sin living in me. ... For in my inner being I delight in God's law; but I see another law at work in me, waging war against the law of my mind and making me a prisoner of the law of sin at work within me."[104] *This is the way the Apostle Paul describes the conflict he experienced. James places this in a relational understanding: "What causes fights and quarrels among you? Don't they come from your desires that battle within you?"*[105] *Relational issues arise from what is within.*

The Apostle Paul acknowledged that,

"... we had no rest, but we were harassed at every turn— conflicts on the outside, fears within."[106]

This was descriptive of his experience. Paul's description of himself was that he was downcast, what we, today, would call depressed. Part of the complexity of relating to others arises from within, from without, and from the weariness of the body or depression. We have all experienced the reality that our relationships are compounded by the extent of our weariness. As parents our frustration explodes in anger often when we are tired and distraught. The interplay of all of these makes it difficult for us to be constant in inviting others to live.

Another behaviour that most of us find disconcerting occurs when a person we are seeking to relate to becomes silent. The wisdom of Ecclesiastes tells us that there is

"... a time to be silent, and a time to speak, ..."[107]

We do not always have that wisdom. The use of silence is a significant skill. However, we must not overlook the fact that silence is powerful and speaks volumes. It may be used positively or negatively. In its appropriate time, such as when one is grieving, it is much more powerful than speech. Presence is sometimes more powerful when shared in silence. Speech may be disruptive. Stillness in silence exudes peace and quietness. It is not demanding of response or interaction. It conveys acceptance, love, and is gentle. Silence may be an invitation to participation. Silence may enable us to hear the quiet whisper of God as Elijah did. It may create a breathing space for contemplation. On the other hand, if silence is the "silent treatment," it may be very painful. It evidences withdrawal, anger, or rejection. It leaves us in a state of ambiguity and wonder not knowing what to do. It creates real possibilities of misinterpretation or false assumptions. It can be a very cruel way to leave an issue of importance. Inattention may be a form of silence expressing a lack of care. The wisdom to know when to speak or be silent is very important.

||||||||||||||||||||||||||||||||||||||||||||||||||||||||||||||||||||||||||||||||||||||||

Nobody said relating effectively was easy.

||||||||||||||||||||||||||||||||||||||||||||||||||||||||||||||||||||||||||||||||||||||||

The Power for the Art

We cannot navigate relationships without addressing the desires and inner drive toward sin. Putting it as simply as possible, the sinful tendencies within mankind must be addressed. The Christian answer is to seek the forgiveness God offers to us in Christ. Secondly, we must seek the will of God for our lives and the enablement to live the life God desires for us through the enablement of the Holy Spirit. Jesus promised his followers that he would pray the Father to send another Comforter who would indwell the believer. Restoration of our relationship with God is the first step to navigating relationships with others.

Our inclination to self-interest, the putting of self before the other person, is one expression of the individualism that has become so dominant in this century. Self-determination has become central in people's thinking. It is related to the sense of entitlement we see today on every hand. There is no effective way to navigate relationships if we do not address these issues. The atomistic person who functions alone does not appear to work in real life experience. Paul recognized this necessity of engaging others with oneself for success and effectiveness. He needed Titus to come alongside to encourage him.[108] The writer of Wisdom in the Old Testament said,

> *"Though one may be overpowered, two can defend themselves.*
> *A cord of three strands is not quickly broken."*[109]

We are bombarded on every side to put self as a priority over everyone else. Submitting ourselves to a higher authority and inviting God into our lives is the most powerful way to rise above self in navigating relationships. The choice is ours. We have that freedom of choice to seek God and his partnership in navigating relationships.

||||||||||||||||||||||||||||||||||||||||||||||||||||||||||||||||||||||||||||||||||||||||

Accessing the help of God enables success.

||||||||||||||||||||||||||||||||||||||||||||||||||||||||||||||||||||||||||||||||||||||||

Enablement requires rising above self-interest. To do so requires assistance. We may receive assistance and affirmation to do so from others. I submit to you that the ultimate enabling to rise above our own interests is best met by a relationship with God. This involves the renewing of the relationship which Adam and Eve lost in rejecting God. As indicated above, God's plan for renewal of that which was lost is found in knowing Christ who came to reveal God to us and to redeem us from that state of separation. In knowing Christ, we are assured of the presence and enablement of the Holy Spirit. The most profound expression of this is found in Paul's writing when he indicates prayer for believers:

> *"I keep asking that the God of our Lord Jesus Christ, the glorious Father, may give you the Spirit of wisdom and revelation, so that you may know him better. I pray that the eyes of your heart may be enlightened in order that you may know the hope to which he has called you, the riches of his glorious inheritance in his holy people, and his incomparably great power for us who believe."*[110]

If you have followed my reasoning through this little book, let me invite you to seek this relationship with God, the Father and enter on this journey of navigating relationship in inviting others to live.

Explore and Interact

1. We are creatures of habit who need to become persons of creativity. Are your habits of communication "invitations to live" or "invitations to die?" If you have the courage, you may wish to ask others for input.

2. Opening ourselves to the helpful input of others is sometimes perceived as a challenge to our individuality and independence. Can you recall and affirm when others have come to your aid? Expressing gratitude is often an important gift to those who help us.

3. Have you explored the interest of God in a relationship with you? This is an adventure worthy of our interest and action.

TIMOTHY'S REFLECTION

He stood over him
Looking down
Chastising
Tormenting
Inviting death
One kneeling answered with silence.
The other yelled
Compelling all who bore witness
To the extended invite.
The one standing asked
For all those who knew
The kneeling man
To save their brother
Their friend
Their belief
Those friends cast
Their wordless invitation
Whispers and screams of
Die die die
Cut through all
Like oil in water
The one kneeling
Offered acceptance
And was
He was beaten, humiliated and crucified.

When he walked
From his own Grave
With his own invite
For all who had offered him
Such hideous death.
He offered a life
Without death
And eternal happiness.
RSVP
Amen.

ENDNOTES

1   Proverbs 18:21

2   Proverbs 30:18

3   John Donne, Meditations: Devotions Upon Emergent Occasions.

4   Julian of Norwich (1343, Revelation of Love (NY: Doubleday, 1997, trans. John Skinner), p. 19

5   Eric Bonhoeffer, Life Together, (NY: Haarper and Row, 1954), p. 77

6   Sydney Jourard, The Transparent Self NY: Van Nostrand Reinhold Co. 1971)pp. 5,15 (italics in original)

7   Roberto Assagioli, Psychosynthesis, (NY: Penguin, 1981), p. 31

8   Genesis 27:38

9   Proverbs 18:21

10   Matthew 12:33-37

11   A. E. Frauenfeld, "Die Macht der Rede, Unser Ville und Weg, August, 1937, pp. 16-21 (source: www.calvin.edu/academic/cas/gpal/machrede. htm,

12   Fredick Buechner, The Hungering Dark (NY: Harper & Row, 1996), p. 46

13   Matthew 12:34

14   Proverbs 12:25

15   Proverbs 15:2

16   Proverbs 16:24

17   Genesis 15:1-4

18   Genesis 45:7-11

19   1 Samuel 23:16-17

20   2 Corinthians 7:3-6

21   Psalm 64:3

22   Job 5:21

23   Proverbs 12:18

24   Psalm 57:4, see also Psalm 64:3; Job 19:2, 5:21; Proverbs 12:18

25   Job 16:3-6

26   Luke 6:44-45

27   Proverbs 10:11, 31; 18:4, 6-8

28   Proverbs 12:18; 15:4; 10:20; 15:2; 16:24; 25:11

29   Proverbs 18:21

30   Proverbs 12:19f

31   Colossians 4:6

32   1 Corinthians 1:5

33   Ephesians 4:29

34   Ephesians 1:18

35   Glenn Tinder, The Fabric of Hope, (MI: Eerdmans, 1999) p. 11

36   Matthew 12:34

37   Roberto Assogioli, The Act of Will, (NY: Viking, 1973, Penguin, 1985)

38   Rod Wilson, Thank you. I'm Sorry. Tell Me More,(NY:NavPress, 2022)

39   Mark 14:3-9

40   Genesi 5:29

41   Philemon 18

42   1 Corinthians 16:18; 2 Timothy 1:16; Philemon 7

43   2 Corinthians 10:5

44   Proverbs 11:9

45   Proverbs 12:18

46   roverbs 15:1

47   Romans 3:13

48   Psalm 10:7

49   Psalm 12:2

50   Psalm 55:20-21

51   Psalm 59:7

52   Psalm 64:3

53   Psalm 64:4

54   Psalm 140:3

55   Job 18:1-5

56   Job 19:2

57   John 9:1-34

58   Psalm 55:12-14

59   Psalm 41:9

60   Mitch Albom, The Five People You Meet in Heaven, (NY: Hyperion 2003) p. 104

61   Henri Nouwen, The Wounded Healer (NY: Doubleday, 1979)

62   Colin Jarman, The Guinness Book of Poisonous Quotes (London: Guinness Publishing, 1991, 1992)

63   Randy Alcorn, Happiness (Ill: Tyndale House Publishing, 2015), p. 26

64   Grant Mullen, Emotionally Free, (MI: Chosen Books; Baker Publishing, 2003) p. 11

65   www.xroado.virginia.edu/-cap/holo/elieebio.htm

66   See two books: Glenn Taylor & Rod Wilson, Exploring Your Anger & Helping Angry People,(BC: Regent College Publishing, 2033)

67   Numbers 13:26-33

68   Matthew 13

69   Matthew 26:36-45

70   Daniel 3

71   Rev. Reid Cooke, Chaplain, Christian Lawyers Fellowship, Newsletter, Winter, 2011

72   Romans 7:15-18

73   Romans 7:25

74   Genesis 2:18

75   Hilary Clinton, It Takes a Village, (NY: Simon & Schuster, 1996)

76   Shaffer & Amundsen, Creating Community Anywhere (Tarcher/Perigree Books, 1993) p. 5, 15

77   Ibid, p. 55

78   Clinton, op cit, p. 7

79   Quoted in Mark Lee, Our Children Are Our Best Friends, (MI: Zondervan, 1972, p. 55

80   Maurice Friedman quoted in Shaffer & Amundson, op cit, p. 86

81   Philippians 2:21

82   Galatians 6:2

83   Romans 15:2

84   1 Corinthians 12:15-21

85   Ephesians 2:10

86   Ephesians 3:14-19; 4:1

87   1 Corinthians 12

88   1 Corinthians 5:17

89 Matthew 6:33

90 Ephesians 1:17-19

91 Philippians 2:1-13

92 Romans 5:5

93 1 John 3:16

94 Matthew 5:43-44

95 Galatians 5:22

96 Romans 12:2

97 James 1:26

98 James 2:8

99 Hebrews 1:1-2

100 Hebrews 4:15

101 Genesis 3:12-13

102 Judges 21:25

103 Psalm 36:2-3

104 Romans 7:14-25

105 James 4:1

106 2 Corinthians 7:5

107 Ecclesiastes 3:7

108 2 Corinthians 7:5-7

109 Ecclesiastes 4:12

110 Ephesians 1:17-19

ABOUT THE AUTHOR

My Christian experience began in my mid-teens. Upon completing Secondary School, I went to seminary to prepare to be a Sunday School teacher. My years in ministry began during my seminary training.

My ministry has been very varied over the past sixty plus years. I pioneered and pastored three churches, served several years as a Correctional Chaplain, and fifteen years in Bible College teaching and administration. During those years, I became involved in serving missionary organizations in psychological testing, orientation, consulting, counselling in over 30 countries. The opportunity to work on a research team for fifteen years studying the impact of missionary ministry on families and single persons was a highlight for me. For over seven years, I administered a large inner-city ministry. The opportunity to serve as president of my denomination and to provide counselling to churches and pastors in difficulty provided much fulfillment.

Academically, I had much opportunity, completing three degrees in theology, two in psychology and several years in post-graduate study. Being certified as a clinical psychologist, I did much psychological testing and assessment. Studies in stress management, trauma intervention and consultation in problem solving and leadership issues gave me a rather multi-disciplinary approach. My ministry was enhanced by working within a medical and psychiatric model. I became quite interested in the neurological impact of trauma and stress on people in ministry. My passion has been to integrate the best I could find in psychology and psychiatry with the grounding of good evangelical theological training.

My wife has participated fully in my ministry for over sixty years and has kept me focused and grounded. My children were also involved in my ministry both in Canada and overseas until they became engaged in their own vocational pursuits. The strength of my family has enabled me to continue in ministry into my eighties with enthusiasm and in the security of their love. I am grateful to the Lord for his sustaining grace during a wonderful experience of service.

BOOKS BY GLENN CALVIN TAYLOR

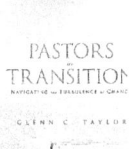

PASTORS IN TRANSITION
SERVANTS OF GOD CHANGE MINISTRIES!
People move to new ministries often. Navigating the turbulence of change is stressful whether within one's culture or to a new culture.

Maximizing growth through change is a key to successful transition. (Word Alive Press, 2013)

Available: wordalivepress.com; Amazon – Paperback or Ebook

THE WEB OF LIFE
SERVANTS OF GOD MINISTER IN COMMUNITIES OF FAITH!
Community is about relationships. Relationships build faith or destroy faith. The life I touch for good or ill touches another, and another!

How do we maximize the strength of community to accomplish God's purposes and His Kingdom? (Word Alive Press, 2016)

Available: wordalivepress.com; Amazon – Paperback or Ebook

FRUITFUL BOUGHS BROKEN
SERVANTS OF GOD IN MINISTRY FACE FAILURE!
This was a reality in the lives of Biblical servants of God, even those models of faith! Failures (big & small) are a reality in fruitful ministries. Failure is never intended, planned, chosen, or expected. Is there forgiveness following failure? (Word Alive Press, 2019)

Available: wordalivepress.com; Amazon – Paperback or Ebook

FINISHING STRONG
SERVANTS OF GOD DESIRE TO FINISH STRONG IN MINISTRY!
The challenges of ministry are often overwhelming. These wilderness experiences impact us physically, emotionally, mentally, confuse our thinking, and drain our spiritual strength. This Biblical and multidisciplinary approach looks at the big picture. What can we learn in the wilderness experiences in ministry? What is God teaching us? Can we know Him in these experiences?

Available: Amazon – Paperback or Ebook

HELPING ANGRY PEOPLE
A SHORT-TERMED STRUCTURED MODEL FOR PASTORAL COUNSELORS
This book is part of a series with David Benner coauthored by Glenn Taylor and Rod Wilson. This is for pastoral counsellors, (Regent College Publishing, 2003)

Available: Amazon – Paperback or Ebook

EXPLORING YOUR ANGER
FRIEND OR FOE?
This book is for the counselled to guide through counselling that involves issues of anger. (Regent College Publishing, 2003)

Available: Amazon – Paperback or Ebook

READ THIS!

Thank you for considering "Navigating Relationships for Life" This book is a distillation of my counselling ministiry ministry to many thousands of people over 60 years. It is one of a complete series "The Navigating Life Series." The other books in the series deal with various aspects of creating a truly successful life!

As a bonus I want to send you a complimentary resources on "Identifying and Managing Your Stress." It will take you less than 20 minutes to read. You can't get this anywhere else!

And it is FREE.

All you need to do is go to GlennCTaylor.ca/stress and tell us where to send it!

HTTPS://GLENNCTAYLOR.CA/STRESS

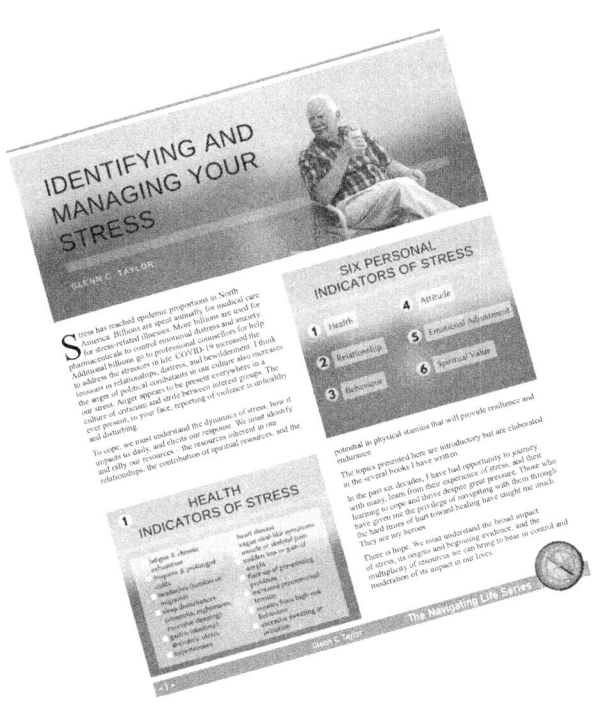

WHAT READERS ARE SAYING

Glenn Taylor's writing on the subject of healthy relationships is the outcome of his educational background, commitment to the church, years of experience in counselling and consulting, biblical and theological convictions, as well as a lifelong commitment to living fully into all aspects of life. As a result, this book has deep roots and a solid foundation. I commend it to you.

Dr. Rod Wilson, Retired President, Regent College, Vancouver, B.C.

There is no substitute for a first hand witness. This is as true today as it was for the Resurrection. This book is the direct result of a truly empathic faithful witness from Glenn Taylor in literally thousands of hours of counsel with the recipients of either the use or misuse of human speech, of damage or repair, and indeed of "living or dying" as he eloquently puts it, in our relational interactions. This is a must read for anyone who is involved in ministry, counseling or leadership of any kind.

James Tughan, Executive Director, Semaphore Fellowship International, Artist, Oakville, Ontario

Glenn is the master of inviting those in his presence to live. In fact, days later you will continue pondering what he has said. As he weaves the web of nurturing others in the community of faith you, too, will be pondering this thoughtful, insightful, handbook in positively influencing others.

Rev. David Johnson, Pastor, Hawkstone, Ontario

Some writers have the special ability to combine academic research with practical experience – and exceedingly powerful combination. Glenn accomplishes this goal in his book, "Navigating Relationships." I especially enjoyed the analogy of the spider web as a strong reminder that my life continues to impact others, just as my life continues to be impacted by others, either in enriching or damaging ways. No relationship is neutral; each touch sets the web in motion. In all of my relational connections with Glenn, his enriching impact through modeling these principles have improved my life and developed my understanding of the power of my words within the structures of communication. I believe the chapter on the importance of the community of faith as a place for receiving love, nurture, and healing meets a critical need in our disconnected society. I highly recommend this book to anyone who wants to improve their relationship quotient.

Marvin Brubacher, Executive Director, MentorLink, Cambridge, Canada

Printed in Great Britain
by Amazon

41532882R00050